NEW CENTURY BIBLE COMMENTARY

General Editors

RONALD E. CLEMENTS	MATTHEW BLACK
(Old Testament)	(New Testament)

JAMES, JUDE, 2 PETER

THE NEW CENTURY BIBLE COMMENTARIES

EXODUS (J. P. Hyatt)
DEUTERONOMY (A. D. H. Mayes)
1 and 2 CHRONICLES (H. G. M. Williamson)
JOB (H. H. Rowley)
PSALMS Volumes 1 and 2 (A. A. Anderson)
ISAIAH 1-39 (R. E. Clements)
ISAIAH 40-66 (R. N. Whybray)
EZEKIEL (John W. Wevers)
THE GOSPEL OF MATTHEW (David Hill)
THE GOSPEL OF MARK (Hugh Anderson)
THE GOSPEL OF LUKE (E. Earle Ellis)
THE GOSPEL OF JOHN (Barnabas Lindars)
THE ACTS OF THE APOSTLES (William Neil)
ROMANS (Matthew Black)
1 and 2 CORINTHIANS (F. F. Bruce)
GALATIANS (Donald Guthrie)
EPHESIANS (C. Leslie Mitton)
PHILIPPIANS (Ralph P. Martin)
COLOSSIANS AND PHILEMON (Ralph P. Martin)
THE PASTORAL EPISTLES (A. T. Hanson)
1 PETER (Ernest Best)
JAMES, JUDE, 2 PETER (E. M. Sidebottom)
THE BOOK OF REVELATION (G. R. Beasley-Murray)

Other titles are in preparation.

NEW CENTURY BIBLE COMMENTARY

Based on the Revised Standard Version

JAMES, JUDE, 2 PETER

E. M. SIDEBOTTOM

WM. B. EERDMANS PUBL. CO., GRAND RAPIDS

MARSHALL, MORGAN & SCOTT PUBL. LTD., LONDON

© Thomas Nelson & Sons Ltd. 1967
assigned to Marshall, Morgan & Scott 1971
First published 1967
Softback edition published 1982

Printed in the United States of America
for
Wm. B. Eerdmans Publishing Company
255 Jefferson Ave. S.E., Grand Rapids, MI 49503
and
Marshall, Morgan & Scott
1 Bath Street, London EC1V 9LB
ISBN 0 551 01002 9

Library of Congress Cataloging in Publication Data
Sidebottom, E. M.
James, Jude, 2 Peter.

(New century Bible commentary)
Bibliography: p. xi
Includes index.
1. Bible. N.T. James — Commentaries. 2. Bible.
N.T. Jude — Commentaries. 3. Bible. N.T. Peter, 2nd —
Commentaries.
I. Title. II. Title: James, Jude, second Peter. III. Series.
BS2785.3.S5 1982 227'.9 82-7469
ISBN 0-8028-1936-2 (soft) AACR2

CONTENTS

LISTS OF ABBREVIATIONS   vii

BIBLIOGRAPHY   xi

INTRODUCTION TO THE EPISTLE OF JAMES

1 Literary Affinities   3

2 Date   11

3 Authorship   18

COMMENTARY ON THE EPISTLE OF JAMES

The Salutation: 1.1   26

The Place of Trial in the Christian Life and in the Purpose of God: 1.2–17   27

James turns to the Ethical Implications of the Teaching upon God: 1.18–21   32

Doers, not Hearers only: 1.22–2.26   35

Further Moral Exhortations: 3.1–5.12   46

Prayer and Faith: 5.13–18   61

GENERAL INTRODUCTION TO THE EPISTLE OF JUDE AND THE SECOND EPISTLE OF PETER

The Priority of Jude   68

INTRODUCTION TO THE EPISTLE OF JUDE

1 Literary Affinities   72

2 Destination   73

3 External Testimony   75

4 The Heresy Involved   75

5 Use of Pseudepigraphic Books and the Stage of Development of the Heresy   76

6 Internal Evidence   77

7 Authorship   78

COMMENTARY ON THE EPISTLE OF JUDE

The Salutation: 1–2   82

The Intention of the Letter: 3–7   83

Description of the Heretics: 8–16   87

Predictions of the Apostles and Exhortations to Hold the Faith:

17–23   91

Doxology: 24–25   93

INTRODUCTION TO THE SECOND EPISTLE OF PETER

1 Literary Affinities   96

2 Date   98

3 Authorship   99

4 Destination   100

COMMENTARY ON THE SECOND EPISTLE OF PETER

The Salutation: 1.1–2   104

Participation in the Divine Nature and Escape from Corruption:
1.3–11   105

How this is to be Achieved: 5–11   107

Purpose of the Epistle to Recall to the Faith: 1.12–21 108

The False Teachers: 2.1–22   112

Belief in the End of the World: 3.1–13   118

The Life which Looks forward to a New World: 3.14–18   124

Doxology   126

INDEX   127

LISTS OF ABBREVIATIONS

ABBREVIATIONS OF THE BOOKS OF THE BIBLE

OLD TESTAMENT (*OT*)

Gen.	Jg.	1 Chr.	Ps.	Lam.	Ob.	Hag.
Exod.	Ru.	2 Chr.	Prov.	Ezek.	Jon.	Zech.
Lev.	1 Sam.	Ezr.	Ec.	Dan.	Mic.	Mal.
Num.	2 Sam.	Neh.	Ca.	Hos.	Nah.	
Dt.	1 Kg.	Est.	Isa.	Jl	Hab.	
Jos.	2 Kg.	Job	Jer.	Am.	Zeph.	

APOCRYPHA (*Apoc.*)

1 Esd.	Tob.	Ad. Est.	Sir.	S. 3 Ch.	Bel	1 Mac.
2 Esd.	Jdt.	Wis.	Bar.	Sus.	Man.	2 Mac.
			Ep. Jer.			

NEW TESTAMENT (*NT*)

Mt.	Ac.	Gal.	1 Th.	Tit.	1 Pet.	3 Jn
Mk	Rom.	Eph.	2 Th.	Phm.	2 Pet.	Jude
Lk.	1 C.	Phil.	1 Tim.	Heb.	1 Jn	Rev.
Jn	2 C.	Col.	2 Tim.	Jas	2 Jn	

ABBREVIATIONS REFERRING TO DEAD SEA SCROLLS

1QIs^a	First Isaiah Scroll
1QIs^b	Second Isaiah Scroll
1QLevi	Second Testament of Levi
1QpHab	Habakkuk Commentary
1QS	Rule of the Community (Manual of Discipline)
1QSa (=1Q28a)	Rule of the Community (Appendix)
1Qsb (=1Q28b)	Collection of Benedictions

1QM	War of the Sons of Light against the Sons of Darkness
1QH	Hymns of Thanksgiving
CD	Fragments of a Zadokite work (Damascus Document)

THE TESTAMENTS OF THE TWELVE PATRIARCHS

These are abbreviated as *Test. Jud.* etc.

RABBINIC WORKS

Targ.	Targum
Tanh.	Tanhuma Midrash on the Pentateuch
Sifre Dt.	Sifre on Deuteronomy

The parts of the Midrash Rabba are listed as *Gen. Rab.* (for Genesis Rabba) etc.

THE MISHNAH

Tractates quoted include

Ber.	Berakoth
Erub.	Erubin
Meg.	Megilla
Yeb.	Yebamoth
Keth.	Kethuboth
Bab. K.	Baba Kamma
Sanh.	Sanhedrin
Sheb.	Shebuoth
Zeb.	Zebahin

A prefixed 'p' indicates the *Jerusalem* Talmud.

OTHER JEWISH WRITINGS

Aristeas	The Epistle of Aristeas
1 Enoch	The 'Ethiopic Book of Enoch'
2 Enoch	'Slavonic Enoch', or The Book of the Secrets of Enoch

Josephus, *Ant.*	*The Antiquities of the Jews*, by Flavius Josephus
Philo, *Leg. All.* etc.	Various works of Philo of Alexandria
Jubil.	The Book of Jubilees
Test. Abr.	The Testament of Abraham, edited by Box

EARLY CHRISTIAN AUTHORS

1 Clem.	The (so-called) First Epistle of Clement of Rome to the Corinthians
2 Clem.	The (so-called) Second Epistle of Clement of Rome to the Corinthians
Clem. Alex. *Strom.* *Protrept.*	The *Stromata* and *Protrepticus* of Clement of Alexandria
Eusebius, *H.E.*	*Historia Ecclesiastica* by Eusebius
Hermas, *Shepherd, Mand.*	Mandates
Sim.	Similitudes
Vis.	Visions
Hippolytus, *Refut.*	Hippolytus' *Refutatio Omnium Haeresium*
Ignatius, *Eph.* *Trall.*	The Epistles of Ignatius to the Ephesians and Trallians
Irenaeus, *Adv. Haer.*	Irenaeus' *Adversus Haereses*
Justin, 1 *Apol.*	The First Apology of Justin
Tertullian, *Apol.* *Ad Scap.*	Tertullian's *Apologeticus* and *ad Scapulam*

FURTHER ABBREVIATIONS

A-NCL	Ante-Nicene Christian Library
AV	Authorized (or King James) Version
CGT	*Cambridge Greek Testament*
CH	Corpus Hermeticum
Charles	*The Apocrypha and Pseudepigrapha of the Old Testament in English*, vol. ii, edited by R. H. Charles
DSS	Dead Sea Scrolls
HNT	Lietzmann, *Handbuch zum NT*
ICC	*International Critical Commentary*

LXX	Septuagint
Migne *PG*	*Patrologiae Cursus Completus* (the Greek Fathers), edited by Migne
MNTC	Moffatt NT Commentary
NEB	New English Bible
Oxyr.	Oxyrhynchus
RSV	Revised Standard Version
RV	Revised Version
S–B, or Billerbeck	*Kommentar zum Neuen Testament aus Talmud und Midrasch*, by Strack and Billerbeck
TWzNT	*Theologisches Wörterbuch zum Neuen Testament*, edited by Kittel

BIBLIOGRAPHY

The Epistle of James

Dibelius   M. Dibelius, *Der Brief des Jakobus*, with supplement by H. Greeven.

Hort   F. J. A. Hort, *The Epistle of St. James* (to 4.7).

Mayor   J. B. Mayor, *The Epistle of St. James*.

Ropes   J. H. Ropes, *St. James, ICC*.

Spitta   F. Spitta, *Der Brief des Jakobus*.

Windisch   H. Windisch, *Die Katholischen Briefe, HNT*.

The Epistle of Jude and the Second Epistle of Peter

Bigg   C. Bigg, *St. Peter and St. Jude, ICC*.

James   M. R. James, *The Second Epistle of Peter and the Epistle of Jude, CGT*.

Mayor   J. B. Mayor, *The Epistle of St. Jude and the Second Epistle of St. Peter*.

Moffatt   J. Moffatt, *The General Epistles: James, Peter and Jude, MNTC*.
Various English translations of the Dead Sea Scrolls are available,
e.g. T. H. Gaster, *The Scriptures of the Dead Sea Sect;* G. Vermes, *The Dead Sea Scrolls in English*; selections in Millar Burrows, *The Dead Sea Scrolls*. The most serviceable translations of 1QpHab and 1QS are by W. H. Brownlee in *The Bulletin of the American Schools of Oriental Research, 112*, pp. 8–18, and *Supplementary Studies, 10–12*.

INTRODUCTION TO THE EPISTLE OF JAMES

The Epistle of James does not resemble a letter except in the salutation, 'James . . . to the twelve tribes in the Dispersion, greeting', and some have believed that even this was a later addition. It is true that the classical epistle was a more formal composition than the ordinary product of correspondence; Cicero often sent round copies of letters he received, and the New Testament shows that Paul adopted the practice of having his letters read in more than one church (Col. 4.16). Epistles in the Roman world were often 'open' letters intended for a wide public and even for posterity. On the Jewish side an example of such a production is the Epistle of Aristeas, the long work purporting to describe the circumstances in which the Septuagint version of the Old Testament originated. Nothing in the New Testament corresponds to this self-conscious literary interest, at least in epistle form. The nearest approach in pre-Christian literature to Paul's epistles are those of Epicurus, which have the same warm expressions of affection, the same purpose of explaining the writer's position, and the same design of holding together the groups practising the way of life he preached: in Epicurus' case, of friendship and blessed freedom from fear. But the Epistle of James resembles none of these. It has no proper introduction, picking up the threads of a previous correspondence or expressing goodwill at the beginning of a new; it contains no reference to matters of common interest; no greetings to particular persons come at the end; and it stops abruptly and without warning. The salutation is not even so explicit as the proems to the Gospel of Luke and the Acts of the Apostles, or the Epistle to Diognetus.

James is in reality a tract showing traces of the diatribe form. The diatribe was a designedly unsystematic address, originating with the Cynics and best known to us in the works of Epictetus. It apparently became the stock-in-trade of the wandering philosopher, and may have influenced the style of exhortation in the synagogue. Ropes gives a list of characteristic traits which are reproduced in James. There is the dialogue with an imaginary interlocutor, 2.18f., 'But some one will say.' With 5.13f., 'is any one among you suffering? . . . is any cheerful?' etc., compare the parallel from the Cynic Teles:

'Are you old? Do not seek the things of youth. Are you ill? Do not seek what belongs to the strong. Are you destitute? Do not seek the life of the well-to-do.' (This is, of course, closer to Paul: 'Are you bound to a wife? Do not seek to be free. Are you free from a wife? Do not seek marriage': 1 C. 7.27; and current maxims probably have at least as much to do with the content of his advice as his eschatological expectations.) The following formulas also have parallels exact or close: 'Do not be deceived. (1.16); 'Do you want to be shown?' (2.20); 'You see' (2.22) and the plural in 2.24; 'know' (1.19); 'what does it profit?' (2.14, 16); 'this ought not to be' to introduce a conclusion; 'behold' (3.4, 5; 5.4, 7, 9, 11). Other characteristics shared by James and the diatribes are: transitions by means of an objection (2.8), a question (2.14; 4.1; 5.13) or 'come' (4.13; 5.1); numerous impera-tives (60 in 108 verses); rhetorical questions; attacks upon *classes* of persons (e.g. the traders and the rich, 4.13–5.6) which do not imply that they are expected to be among the readers; the conventional comparisons of the rudder, the bridle, the forest fire (3.3–6); the stock instances of famous individuals (here Abraham, Rahab, Job, Elijah); the harsh mode of address ('empty head' 2.20; 'adultereresses' 4.4); the characteristic methods of framing sections and using key-words to tie a passage together, as 'temptation' in 1.2–14, 'wisdom' in 3.13–18, 'zeal' in 3.13–4.2, 'bridle the tongue' in 1.26; 3.2, 'word' in 1.18–23, 'law of freedom' in 1.25; 2.12, 'judge' in 4.11, 12. Ropes finds similar themes also in James and the diatribes. He recognizes that the various traits can be individually paralleled in other types of literature, and he notes the greater seriousness, restraint, and kindli-ness of James, who also addresses his readers not as discrete individuals but as members of the common brotherhood: 'My brethren'. But it is generally agreed that the case for comparison with the diatribe has been made out.

Dibelius, however, pointed out that the loose construction and grouping of sayings in James pointed to an origin in early Christian hortatory instruction, and research into the forms of ethical instruc-tion used in the New Testament has led to the classification of James with specifically Christian patterns of teaching which grew up from Christian origins. This is indeed in keeping with the observation that the teaching of Jesus as collected in the so-called Sermon on the Mount and his apostrophizing of the scribes and Pharisees, especially as it is delineated by Matthew, is not unlike James and shares some of the characteristics of the diatribe enumerated above. It has been noticed that when the New Testament writers turn to ethical exhortation they display a remarkable identity of style. Dodd has challenged readers to assign 1 Th. 5.14-18, Heb. 13.1-3, and 1 Pet. 3.8-9 to context on grounds of style alone (*Gospel and Law*, pp. 18f.). It is pointed out that the style encountered in the lists of virtues (Gal. 5.22f.; 1 Tim. 6.11; 2 Pet. 1.5-7), vices (Rom. 1.29-31; 13.13; 1 C. 5.10f.), and exhortations (Col. 3.18ff.) is markedly different from that employed elsewhere in the documents in which they are embedded (though the predominance of the imperative mood renders this not altogether surprising), and it has been suggested that they draw upon conventional Hellenistic morality. There is obviously more than this, however, to such a passage as Gal. 5.22 included above, and Carrington and Selwyn have sought to lay a foundation for the study of New Testament ethical teaching in a way which fully allows for its Christian provenance. They have sought to show that a primitive Christian 'Holiness Code' recalling Lev. 17-26 crops up in places like 1 Th. 4.1-12; 1 C. 6.1-11; 1 Pet. 1.15ff.; 2.12, etc., and that it was used in pre-baptismal catechism. Such hortatory material usually follows upon doctrinal exposition, and here 'usually' means in effect in the Pauline epistles, since these and their imitations form the bulk of the New Testament. James is often included in tables of such material, but clearly much more work must be done before it is possible to be dogmatic about exact forms, and allowance has to be made for the existence of variations. It may be suspected that James presents a more complicated problem than can be solved by regarding it as the hind end of a Pauline epistle, if only for the fact that moral exhortation is here separate from distinctive Christian dogma and from the desire to link it with the example of Jesus, as elsewhere in the New Testament—though in Hebrews a combination of the two types occurs.

1. LITERARY AFFINITIES

The Epistle of James, whatever its form, is to be understood against the background of first-century Judaism. There are few parallels in rabbinic writings except in the most general sense; for example, that the man who stands firm in trial is blessed (Jas 1.2; *Exod. Rab.* 31), or that it is good to pursue peace (Jas 3.18; *Aboth* 1.12), preserve silence (Jas 1.19; 2.14ff.; *Aboth* 1.17), and not plan too assiduously for the future (Jas 4.13ff.; *Ber.* 9b), or that God exalts those who humble themselves, and vice versa (*Erub.* 13b). Parallels to such conventional maxims can be found in secular writers such as Seneca, and in Philo and the Wisdom writers. James represents a different style from that of the rabbis.

It cannot be said that the Dead Sea Scrolls are much nearer. It is difficult to read the notion of the eschatological *peirasmos* into the trials of Jas 1.12 (cf. 1QS 8.4; 1QH 2.35; 9.6ff.; 8.26ff.; 11.19ff.) The diadem of glory and robe of beauty in 1QS 4.7f. are nearer to Wis. 5.16ff.; 18.24, and the imagery recurs in the Odes of Solomon 1 (the Odes, like James and the Dead Sea Scrolls, being influenced by Wisdom phraseology). In 1QS 3.20 control over the 'sons of righteousness' is 'in the hand of the Prince of Lights' (cf. Jas 1.17). The Qumran doctrine of the two spirits is discovered in 4.5, and the dualism of bad and good in 3.11 (cf. 1QS 3.19). Attention is drawn to the notes on these passages. Neither James nor the Covenanters set much store by the possession of wealth (Jas 2.2–4).

The conventional character of much of James is shown by the numerous resemblances discoverable in contemporary and relatively recent literature such as Proverbs, ben Sirach, the Book of Wisdom, the Epistle of Aristeas, Philo of Alexandria, and so on. The following are some examples:

Jas 1.5, God gives Wisdom=Prov. 2.6; Sir. 1.3ff.

Jas 1.7f., prayer with a double heart=Prov. 1.28.

Jas 1.9, the lowly brother=Prov. 28.6.

Jas 1.9, cf. 4.6, humility=Aristeas 263; Sir. 3.18; Prov. 3.34.

Jas 1.19, be slow to anger=Ec. 7.9.

Jas 1.19, be swift to hear=Sir. 5.11.

Jas 3 resembles Wis. 5.6–15 in some respects.

Jas 3.2, on not erring in speech= Sir. 14.1.

Jas 3.6, the tongue a fire= Sir. 5.13; cf. Prov. 16.27, esp. LXX; Sir. 5.10–6.1; 32.4, 7–9.

Jas 3.17f. resembles Wis. 7.22ff. in style and tone.

Jas 3.18, fruits of righteousness= Aristeas 233 (cf. 260); Prov. 11.30; cf. Am. 6.12; Phil. 1.11; Heb. 12.11.

Jas 4.1, self-indulgence, ease, and pleasure= Aristeas 245, 277; 4 Mac. 1.20ff.

Jas 4.6, God opposes the proud and gives grace to the humble= Aristeas 257, 263; Prov. 3.34; cf. 1 Sam. 2.7f.; Lk. 1.51f.

Jas 4.13f., not knowing what the morrow will bring= Prov. 27.1; cf. Sir. 10.10; 11.19.

Jas 4.13, gain= Aristeas 270.

Jas 5.6, theme of righteous persons= Wis. 2.12–20.

Jas 5.12, avoiding oaths= Sir. 23.9ff.; 27.14; Philo: *De Decal.* 17–19; *De Spec. Leg.* 2:1ff.

Jas 5.14ff., praying and confessing in sickness= Sir. 38.9f.

Jas 5.17, Elijah honoured for stopping famine= Sir. 48.2f.

Jas 5.20, on covering offences= Prov. 10.12 (but 1 Pet. 4.8 is closer). It would be possible to extend the list indefinitely, especially from the voluminous writings of Philo, and to call upon 1 Enoch and the other apocalyptic books also. Other references are noted in the Commentary. Parallels are also abundant from secular sources.

Closest of all, however, from Jewish literature, and important for reasons which will be clear later, are the *Testaments of the Twelve Patriarchs*, a work probably originally Palestinian and in Hebrew, dating from the second century B.C. but containing additions and probably Christian interpolations. These are some of the important parallels with James, and they show close verbal resemblance:

Jas 1.2–4. Count it all joy, my brethren, when you meet various trials, for you know that the testing of your faith produces steadfastness. And let steadfastness have its full effect, that you may be perfect and complete, lacking in nothing.

2

Test. Jos. 2.7. In ten trials he showed me tested,
              And in all of them I was patient;
              For patience is a mighty remedy,
              And steadfastness gives many good things.
Jas 2.13. For judgment is without mercy to one who has shown no mercy; yet mercy triumphs over judgment.
Test. Zeb. 8.3. For as a man has compassion upon his neighbour, so also the Lord has upon him. (Charles brackets this as a *Jewish* interpolation.)
Jas 3.9f. With it [the tongue] we bless the Lord and Father, and with it we curse men, who are made in the likeness of God. From the same mouth come blessing and cursing. My brethren, this ought not to be so.
Test. Benj. 6.5. The good mind has not two tongues, of blessing and cursing, of insolence and honour, of silence and uproar, of hypocrisy and truth (of poverty and wealth); but it has one disposition, genuine and pure, concerning all men.
Jas 4.7b. Resist the devil and he will flee from you.
Test. Naph. 8.4. And the devil will flee from you.
Jas 4.8. Draw near to God.
Test. Dan 6.2. Draw near to God.

In the New Testament James has a relationship with Romans and Galatians (cf. Jas 1.22 with Rom. 2.13; Jas 4.1 with Rom. 7.23; Jas 2.10 with Gal. 3.10; 5.3), Ephesians and Colossians in the Pauline *corpus*; and outside this with Hebrews and 1 Peter. There are some connections with the Johannine writings. St Matthew's Gospel is also involved. Apart from it, the most striking similarities are with 1 Peter, as the following table shows. It will be useful to have Colossians and Ephesians as controls. Quotations from these and passages from James which refer to them are printed in italics, and the more remote parallels are enclosed in brackets.

James	1 Peter
1.1. to the twelve tribes in the dispersion.	1.1. to the exiles of the dispersion.
1.2. Count it all joy . . . when	1.6. In this rejoice, though now

you meet various trials.	for a little while you may have to suffer various trials.
1.3. the genuine element in your faith.	1.7. the genuine element in your faith.
1.6. *like a wave of the sea driven and tossed by the wind.*	*Eph. 4.14. tossed to and fro and carried about with every wind of doctrine.*
1.10f. he will pass away like the flower of the grass. For the sun . . . withers the grass; its flower falls.	1.24. All flesh is like grass and all its glory like the flower of grass. The grass withers, and the flower falls (Isa. 40.6–9).
(*1.17. Father of lights.*)	(*Eph. 5.8. children of light.*)
1.18. he brought us forth by the word of truth, that we should be a kind of first-fruits of his creatures.	1.3. begotten again to a living hope. 1.23. begotten again not of perishable seed but . . . through the living and abiding word of God.
1.19. *slow to anger.*	
1.21. *put away all filthiness and rank growth of evil (malice).*	*Col. 3.8. put away . . . wrath, anger, evil (malice).*
(1.25. he who looks . . .)	(1.12. angels long to look . . .)
(1.26. general reference to refraining tongue.)	(3.10.)
(2.7. honourable name.)	
(*3.10. general reference to evil talk.*)	(4.14. name of Christ.)
(3.13. general reference to good deeds.)	(*Eph. 4.29.*)
	(2.12.)
3.14. *bitterness to be put away.*	*Eph. 4.31.*
4.7. submit yourselves to God.	5.6. humble yourselves under the mighty hand of God.
4.7. resist the devil.	5.8f. resist the devil.
5.3. your gold and silver have rusted.	1.18. perishable things such as silver and gold.
(*5.13. reference to singing psalms.*)	(*Eph. 5.19.*)
5.20. will cover a multitude of sins.	4.8. love covers a multitude of sins (Prov. 10.12).

The relationship between the two writings is an extraordinary one. They are alike in phraseology and some ideas, yet different in thought. This similarity is more than can be wholly explained by the assumption of a common stock of phrases over a wide area and a long time, and more must be said upon this point in the discussion of the date.

In the margin of James in the Nestle Greek Testament there are twenty-six references to 1 Peter, while to Colossians, for example, there are only eight; and we remember that James is supposed to have a special affinity with the teaching-pattern of Colossians. But the references to Matthew amount to thirty-eight, a quarter of all references to all books of the Bible and Apocrypha, and those recorded by no means cover all the possible parallels. The following list only includes the obvious ones, and omits some given by Nestle. Luke, Mark, and Hebrews are used as controls.

James	Matthew
1.2. Count it joy . . . when you meet various trials.	5.10ff. Blessed are you, when men persecute you.
1.4. perfect and complete, lacking nothing.	5.48. perfect as your Father. 19.21. If you would be perfect cf. Mk 10.21. You lack one thing.
1.5f. It will be given him: let him ask in faith.	7.7. ask and it will be given you, cf. Mk 11.22ff.
1.6. in faith with no doubting.	21.21. if you have faith and never doubt.
1.11. grass withers when sun rises.	13.6. similar wording in the Sower.
1.12. Blessed is the man who endures trial.	cf. 5.10ff. above.
1.17. every good gift is from above, from the Father of lights.	7.11. Your Father in heaven will give good things; cf. Lk. 11.13.
1.19. slow to anger.	5.22. everyone who is angry.
1.21. receive the implanted word which is able to save your souls.	*Lk. 8.11f. The seed is the word of God. The ones along the path are those who have heard; then the devil*

comes and takes away the word from
their hearts, that they may not
believe and be saved.

1.22. doers of the word.

7.21. not everyone who says
Lord, Lord.

7.26. who hears my words and
does not.

(Lk 11.28. hear the word of God
and keep it.)

(Lk. 12.47. who did not do his
master's will.)

1.25. a doer that acts.

7.24. who hears and does; cf.
Lk. 10.37.

(1.27. visit orphans.)
(and widows.)
(2.2 assembly.)

(25.24. you visited me.)
(Mk 12.40. devour widows' houses.)
(Heb. 10.25. assembling.)

2.5. God has chosen the poor.
(rich in faith.)

5.3. Blessed are the poor.
(Lk. 12.21. rich toward God.)

2.8. love your neighbour.

22.39. love your neighbour.

2.10. whoever keeps the whole
law.

5.19. whoever relaxes one commandment.

2.13. judgment is without mercy
to one who has shown no mercy.

5.7. blessed are the merciful: they
shall receive mercy.

18.29, 34. the merciless servant.

25.45f. as you did it not to the
least.

2.14. faith without works.

7.21. not every one who says
Lord, Lord.

21.29. answered, I will not, but
afterwards repented and went.

2.15. brother or sister naked.

25.36. I was naked . . . my
brethren.

2.19. the demons believe.

8.29f. the demons recognise
Christ; cf. Lk. 4.34.

2.21. Abraham offering Isaac.
2.25. Rahab.

Heb. 11.17.
Heb. 11.31.

3.1. Be not many teachers.

23.8. be not called rabbi.

3.2. If any one makes no mistakes in what he says, he is a perfect man.

12.35ff. judged by words.

3.6. tongue a stain.

15.11. what comes out of the mouth defiles a man; cf. verse 18.

3.12. Can a fig tree yield olives?, etc.

7.16. figs from thistles?, etc.

3.17. good fruits.

12.33. make the tree good . . . good fruit.

3.18. making peace.

5.9. peacemakers.

4.3. you ask and do not receive. (4.4. friendship of the world enmity with God.)

7.7. Ask and it will be given you. (6.24. no one can serve two masters.)

4.6. God gives grace to the humble.

Lk. 14.11. who exalts himself will be humbled: Mt. 23.12; Lk. 18.14; Mt. 18.4.

4.9. laughter turned to mourning.
4.10. Humble yourselves before the Lord.

Lk. 6.25. Woe to you that laugh.
cf. Lk. 14.11 above.

4.11. he that judges.
4.12. one judge to save and destroy.

7.1–5. Judge not.
10.28. destroy soul and body.

4.13. today or tomorrow.

6.34. be not anxious for the morrow.

(4.13. get gain.)

(16.26. profit if gain whole world? *cf. Lk. 12.16ff., the Rich Fool.*)

4.17. knowing: and doing not.

Lk. 12.47. servant who knew and did not.

5.1. rich men, weep and howl.
5.2. your riches have rotted, etc.
5.3. your gold and silver.
5.5. you have lived on the earth in luxury and pleasure.

Lk. 6.24. woe to rich.
6.19. moth and rust consume.
10.9. take no gold nor silver.
Lk. 16.19, 25. The rich man in purple: 'In your lifetime good things.'

(5.7. Be patient.)

(Lk. 21.19. by your patience.)
(Heb. 10.36. you need patience.)

(5.7. *parousia* likened to harvest.) (Parables in Mt. 13; cf. Mk 4.) The word *parousia* is peculiar to Matthew in the Gospels.

5.9. judge stands at the door. 24.33. He is near, at the gates; in Mk 13.29 the kingdom is probably meant; the 'he' is rendered plausible by the proximity of verse 27, originally distinct; cf. Lk. 21.31.

5.10. prophets as example. 5.12. persecuted prophets.

5.11. Count happy those who endure. 10.22. he who endures to the end.

5.12. do not swear. 5.34. do not swear.

(*5.14. anointing the sick.*) (*Mk 6.13.*)

The notes contain further parallels. They do not show the same striking verbal similarities as those between James and 1 Peter, but show a similarity of concern and a familiarity with the recorded teaching of Jesus unique in the New Testament, and moreover with that tradition of the teaching that is peculiar to Matthew. Moreover, as we have noted already, despite the prominent traces of diatribe form, James' style is also like that of the Sermon on the Mount and the denunciations of the scribes and Pharisees.

2. DATE

EXTERNAL EVIDENCE

Outside the New Testament there are no obvious references to James at all before the end of the second century. It is possible to find parallels enough to the sentiments expressed, just as it was possible to find numerous parallels in the Jewish and secular literature. Examples are either too general or else concern too exclusively mere verbal similarities to deserve mention, with the exception of one or two which involve the question of the date of James. Of these the two documents usually involved are the *Shepherd* of Hermas and the (first) Epistle of Clement of Rome to the Corinthians, usually dated 130–145 and 90 respectively. A third is the *Didache*, or Teaching of the Twelve Apostles, now that the fashion of dating it late is passing here. On the Continent it has always been regarded as early, and the latest commentator, J. P. Audet, sets it as early as A.D. 60. This work resembles James in many points of teaching: renunciation of anger and partiality and double-mindedness, for example. The first six chapters are based apparently on a Jewish moral code called the Two Ways, which is also used in the last part of the so-called Epistle of Barnabas, and has the same affinities with Leviticus as have been discovered in New Testament parenesis. In style, with its repeated 'My child' it recalls more clearly the Book of Proverbs than James does. The *Shepherd* of Hermas also has a primitive atmosphere which, apart from the statement of the Muratorian Canon that it was written 'recently, in our times' (i.e. late second century), would place it early also. (The description of the circumstances surrounding the composition of John's Gospel does not inspire any great confidence in the credibility of the Muratorian Canon. According to this, John told his associates to fast so that they could relate to each other any visions they might have, and thus it was revealed to Andrew that they should certify what John wrote.)

Hermas himself claims a date contemporary with Clement of Rome, and the solution has been suggested that his tract was written over a period of thirty or forty years.

Both Hermas and the *Didache* use the adjective *dipsychos* 'double-minded' (Jas 1.8) which does not occur in extant writings before James (it appears once in a fragment as the title of a work by Philo, but does not seem to be by his hand) and becomes popular afterwards, e.g. in Clement of Rome, 11.2; 23.3. The last passage quotes it in an extract from what is called 'scripture' and it is repeated in the pseudonymous 2 Clem. 11.2 as 'the prophetic word'. This 'scripture' or 'prophetic word' appears to be a work called 'The Book of Eldad and Modad' based on Num. 11.26–29. The word for 'double-minded' occurs in the part of Hermas which would be earliest on the theory that it was written over a number of years (*Vis.* 3.4), but soon before (*Vis.* 2.3) the Book of Eldad and Modad, 'who prophesied to the people in the wilderness' is quoted (cf. on Jas 1.8; 4.5, 8; 5.7 below). On this showing, then, *dipsychos* could also be older than James. Nevertheless, the context in which it occurs in

Mand. 9 contains other parallels to James, the section on prayer without double-mindedness and doubting God's readiness to answer, bearing no grudge and so on, being in much the same order as Jas 1.5–8. It must be admitted also that the general atmosphere of James, the *Didache*, and Hermas is of a very early period in the Church's history.

The position with Clement of Rome is somewhat similar. Here again, to be sure, some similarities with James are easily explainable on the basis of common tradition: 1 Clem. 30.2, ' "For God," it says, "resists the proud and gives grace to the humble" ' is a quotation from Prov. 3.34, and so is 1 Pet. 5.5 as well as Jas 4.6. 1 Clem. 49.5 'love covers a multitude of sins' is from Prov. 10.12, and is nearer 1 Pet. 4.8 than Jas 5.20. The LXX term for the twelve tribes of Israel is used in 1 Clem. 31.4 (cf. Jas 1.1 and 1 Pet. 1.1). Abraham and Rahab the harlot occur in Clement (10.1; 12.1) and James (2.23, 25) as examples of faith, but also appear in Heb. (11.8, 31). Moreover, Clement refers in addition to Enoch, Noah, and Lot as well as Abraham and Rahab; Hebrews adds Abel, Sarah, Isaac, Jacob, Joseph, Moses, and a host of others (Heb. 11.4ff.). Yet the impression remains that Clement is nearer to James than the parenetic tradition theory suggests; it is more striking than the coincidences of ideas that the language and order occasionally coincide also. The text from Prov. 3.34 (Jas 4.6) quoted in 1 Clem. 30.2 is followed by a verse which takes up the theme of James that we are 'justified by works and not by words' (Jas 2.14 'says he has faith'; cf. 1.22). Here 'justification' has a treatment typical of James and not of Paul or Jesus (cf. Lk. 18.14). The theme of obedience to God's 'words' occurs again in 1 Clem. 10.1, where Abraham is faithful to the 'words' of God (Jas 1.22) and is moreover 'the Friend of God', as in Jas 2.23. In 1 Clem. 31.2 he is 'our Father Abraham', as in Jas 2.21. Of course, the titles and themes occur elsewhere, but not together, as in these two works.

INTERNAL EVIDENCE

The Epistle of James has strong Jewish elements, which suggest a Palestinian place of origin, and a primitive tone closest to the Synoptic Gospels, with the emphasis upon Jesus' teaching and an

unobtrusive Christology. Mention of the synagogue (2.2 *RSV*
'assembly'), the elders of the church and anointing with oil (5.14)
has a similar early sound. The word 'Gehenna' appears in the New
Testament in transliteration only in Jas 3.6, apart from Jesus' teaching
as recorded in the Synoptics. As in the Synoptics also, the Coming
of the Lord (*parousia*, as in Matthew) is compared with farming
activity (5.7), and the 'kingdom' is introduced (2.5). 'Faith' in 2.14,
etc., is very like that in the Gospels, and the demons shudder as before
the Lord (Jas 2.19; Mk 1.24, 34b, etc.). That some of these features
reappear in later works (Clement, Ignatius, Barnabas) does not
destroy the impression of an almost pre-crucifixion discipleship. Not
only is the person of Jesus left out, his name only introduced at two
points (where it could be omitted without damage to the sense), and
no reference made to cross or resurrection or the events of the
ministry, but his example is ignored, and his teaching left to stand
by its own inherent value. The other place which the undeveloped
theology of James recalls is the opening chapters of Acts.

A further sign of an early date is the lack of warnings against false
teaching or the mythologizing of a nascent gnosticism plus the horror
of the flesh, which occurs in later books of the New Testament. It
is worth remembering that before the end of the second century
James' name was closely associated with gnosticism. The sins and
errors rebuked are typically Jewish, and so is the absence of controversy over matters of doctrine and the emphasis on practice rather
than creed. It may be that James can be explained as a 'fossil'
preservation, as English scholars have been inclined to regard both
the *Didache* and the *Shepherd* of Hermas, but this kind of thing can
be pushed too far.

COMPARISON WITH MATTHEW

The close connection of James with Matthew will be obvious upon
consideration of the above list. Both writers seem to have to do with
a similar type of community: cf. Jas 5.3 with Mt. 10.10, where silver
and gold are added to the copper in Mk 6.8 (the mention in James
is made in a context which recalls Jesus' saying about moth and rust
corrupting, recorded in Mt. 6.19ff.; cf. Lk. 12.33). But if the tradition
underlying Matthew's special source and his way of dealing with

Marcan material was known to James, it was plainly not yet in fixed
form, for although James' version of the sayings is most like
Matthew's, in no case is it identical in language. James also shares
with Matthew a close relationship with *The Testaments of the Twelve
Patriarchs* (for Matthew in this connection see Plummer, *An Exegetical
Commentary on the Gospel According to St Matthew*, xxxiv). No
agreement has been reached over the date of Matthew, but it seems
to have reached its final form after A.D. 70. There is much to be said
for the contention that Matthew was written in Jamnia under the
influence of and in reaction to the school of Johanan ben Zakkai,
after the Jewish war. Certainly, there is a strong rabbinical influence
visible in it; but, if so, the lack of such influence on James points to
an earlier stage of the tradition it shares with the First Gospel. This
would suggest a date for James before A.D. 70, to allow time for the
further developments to take place, and the date might be much
earlier, if (as some indications suggest, e.g. the similar attitude to
enemies as that evinced by Johanan, cf. Mt. 5.39a, 41; 26.52),
Matthew was written not long after A.D. 70.

I PETER

A close relationship is sometimes discerned between James on the
one hand and Hebrews, Colossians, and Ephesians on the other. A
study of the list on pp. 6f. is sufficient to show how much closer is
that between James and 1 Peter. While it is possible to draw comparisons between Col. 3.8–4.12; Eph. 4.20–6.19; 1 Pet. 1.1–4.11;
1 Pet. 4.12–5.14 and Jas 1.1–4.10 and show that they follow the same
order, a completely different comparison in order is possible between
Jas 1.1–21 and 1 Pet. 1.1–2.1, after which only sporadic correspondences occur (e.g. Jas 4.7 with 1 Pet. 5.8f.; Jas 5.20 with
1 Pet. 4.8). This will also be clear from the above list. The relationship between the two is thus on a different footing from that between
Colossians and Ephesians. Moreover, the astonishing verbal correspondences between them are more than can be explained on the
basis of a common store of phrases and conventions possessed by the
synagogue or the Church. But if there is a question of literary
dependence one way or the other, the Epistle of James looks earlier.
Its aphoristic style is more likely to have come first than the more

diffuse manner of 1 Peter: cf. Jas 4.7 with 1 Pet. 5.8ff., and see on Jas 1.9ff. In any case they are so closely connected in the same tradition that the more primitive tone of James suggests for it an earlier date. If then 1 Peter is genuine, this will be before 64 when Peter was martyred. If it is not genuine, of course, no significant conclusion about the date is possible, since those who reject the Petrine authorship do not agree on the date of composition of 1 Peter.

COMPARISON WITH PAUL

The earliest date obtainable from a comparison with other New Testament writers emerges from an examination of the relationship between the teaching of Paul and James on faith and works. That there is a connection between the two is almost certain, for, so far as we know, the notion of justification *by faith alone* occurs only in James 2 and Paul in the whole of Jewish and Christian literature. This is not to say that there was no discussion upon faith and works in Judaism; Philo and the author of 2 Esdras, for example, devote space to it. Nor is the idea of justification by faith original to Paul and James in the New Testament. It occurs in the teaching of Jesus (Mk 2.17b; Lk. 6.20), as does also some of the language: the Aramaizing Greek of Lk. 18.14* shows it to be pre-Pauline. But the exclusive position 'by faith alone' is unique, and seems to originate with Paul: it is to this that James is replying. From what we know of him in his own work, he would have understood and sympathized with the position of those Jewish Christians who were troubled by Paul's apparent antinomianism, so long as they kept to a purely ethical conception of law. On the other hand, it is hard to see how anyone who was directly acquainted with Paul's teaching could offer so incompetent a critique of it. He connects the verse 'Abraham believed God, and it was reckoned to him as righteousness' (Gen. 15.6), quoted also by Paul, with the offering of Isaac, which Paul does not do. Both writers are evidently drawing upon

---

* Especially the underlying *min*, from, in the sense of 'and not': 'this one went down justified *and not* the other'. The passive construction may also reproduce the Jewish avoidance of the divine name, but this is often overdone. Here the passive is sufficient and most effective alone.

traditions in which Abraham is used as an example, but they use the example to prove opposite conclusions without apparently being aware that they are doing so. The two lines of argument, in fact, run parallel without ever touching. Not only would Paul never have countenanced the doctrine that the justified should 'continue in sin', but all the terms involved are used in a different sense by each protagonist. Paul thinks of faith in the inclusive sense of union with Christ; James varies in regarding it now as allegiance (2.1 where he is already speaking of obedience), now as belief in God's power and willingness to help (2.16: ' "Go in peace, be warmed and filled," without giving them the things needed for the body'). 'Works' likewise has a different meaning in each author. For Paul it is the meritorious fulfilment of the whole Law, with special emphasis on its ritual requirements. For James it means acts of Christian love. The two writers are nearer in their use of the term 'to justify'; but even here Paul would never have been forced into the position of saying that a man's works make no difference to his destiny: in Rom. 2.6 he quotes Prov. 24.12b (just as does the evangelist Matthew: Mt. 16.27): 'He will render to every man according to his works,' and he keeps on repeating the sentiment: 1 C. 3.8; 2 C. 5.10. Like James, and moreover at the height of the 'faith-works' controversy, he asks for 'faith that becomes effective through love' (Gal. 5.6). Paul, in fact, in his polemics against reliance on Law, is not opposing moral obedience or even ritual conformity (he advised Jewish Christians to practise Torah and ascribed a new Torah to Christ himself); what he is doing is to contrast the Law and Christ as alternative sources of salvation.

It seems clear that James was not acquainted with any clear or systematic exposition of Paul's thought. It is only necessary to consider Rom. 4.2ff. (cf. Gal. 3) alongside Jas 2.20ff. The two writings seem plainly independent. In Romans (and Gal. 3) Paul is speaking of the relationship with God, which did not begin under the formal auspices of the Law with its initiation ceremony circumcision; James, without any indication that he has ever heard of an argument such as this, is blithely using the same text (Gen. 15.6) to prove something entirely different, namely that faith does not exist unless it expresses itself through works, and in connection with the offering of Isaac, with which it has no connection in the original text of Genesis or in the writings of Paul. There does indeed appear to have been a tradition which used the story of Abraham's offering of Isaac as an instance of faith just as James does, for it occurs in this connection in Hebrews (11.17ff.) and 1 Clement (31.2). It is quite possible that in this respect it is Paul who is out of step; but there seems to be no question that James knew of his teaching, and, unlike the writers of Hebrews and 1 Clement, was sufficiently clear about the question at stake to join issue over it. At the same time he only knew of it in an imprecise way. The conclusion must be that he wrote before Paul's letters clarifying his attitude on this subject achieved wide circulation. Paul was still defending himself on the issue at the time of the writing of Romans, in the middle or late fifties. On this showing, then, we may place James about this time. This agrees with the results of the comparisons with Matthew and 1 Peter. James would thus not be the earliest of all the New Testament writings, as maintained by Kittel, but would be early enough to explain its primitive atmosphere, while at the same time maintaining connections with 1 Peter and the developing special source of Matthew.

Other indications in the epistle point to a similar period. The mention of anxiety about early and late rains seems to indicate Palestine as its place of origin. Absence of illustrations drawn from commercial life (common in diatribes) and references to farming activities suggest the country, as opposed to the town, but the description of the assembly does not give the impression of a small place. The church involved is a settled community even apparently forming a part of Jewish life, and likely to be visited even by the rich who may not be Christians (2.1ff.). The problems mentioned are wholly domestic; no persecution impends; no public catastrophe seems recent or imminent. This makes a date after A.D. 66 highly improbable (see the important remarks of Albright, *Archæology of Palestine*, pp. 240ff., on conditions during and after the war years of 66 onwards and the position of Christians especially). The similarities to the special source of Matthew, plus the absence of references to persecution and controversy with rabbis contained in it, accord with this situation, and suggest a period before the war of A.D. 66. The comparison with 1 Peter and Paul produced the same result.

3. AUTHORSHIP

The epistle is traditionally attributed to James the brother of the Lord, bishop of Jerusalem, not to be confused with the apostle James (the brethren of the Lord were not believers during his lifetime: Mk 3.21, 31; Jn 7.3–9; cf. Ac. 1.13 and 14). The objections to this are: the good Greek of the epistle, its use of the Septuagint version and its Hellenistic flavour; the attitude to the Law, which is not supposed to be that typical of James of Jerusalem; the absence of reference to the problems dealt with at the Council of Jerusalem in Acts 15; and the lateness of any reference to the work in the early Fathers (it is not mentioned before Origen). The weight of most of these objections has been exaggerated. The Greek of the epistle is not of the quality of, say, St Luke's introduction to his Gospel; and it could have been the work of an amanuensis. Moreover, the fact is that we know very little about the penetration of Palestine by Greek culture. It has at least become clearer in recent years that there was no simple progression from Palestinian to Hellenistic Christianity, so that wherever the latter appeared it could be dubbed late or as originating in the Dispersion (see note on 1.1 for the use of 'Dispersion' in our epistle; it evidently is not intended to refer to the Jewish Dispersion as such, even if the ascription is an integral part of the work). The difference between Paul and James over the Law can be exaggerated. The decision of the Council in Acts 15.13–21 presided over by James was a victory for Gentile liberty from the ceremonial requirements of the Law, and ten years later James was still friendly towards Paul, though also trusted by the Jewish Christians 'zealous for the Law' (Ac. 21.18ff.).

Paul confirms this friendly attitude: Gal. 2.9 implies that James recognized the right of Gentiles to be Christians without being circumcised. The tradition which makes the title 'Just' applied to James mean 'ceremonially correct' is legendary. Hegesippus describes (Eusebius, *H.E.* II 23) how this reputation made him acceptable to the Jews, and how he was a Nazirite who wore only linen and had knees calloused like a camel's through kneeling in intercession for the people. But according to Josephus his martyrdom in A.D. 62 was effected on a charge of violating the Law (*Ant. XX*, 9.1). It may also be said, in passing, that Hegesippus's account does not support recent efforts to rehabilitate the traditional authorship by making James a member of the Qumran sect. The latter indulged in numerous ablutions, whereas Hegesippus says that James never used the bath! Dodd concluded that the word 'Law' in the Epistle of James was used exactly as in the writings of Paul, whose 'leanings to the Greek side are more significant than his leanings to the Hebrew side' (*Bible and Greeks*, pp. 39, 41). But it may be assumed that if anything was at issue between Paul and James of Jerusalem it was not the *conception* of Law but how to apply it to Christians. Paul was brought up the strictest of Pharisees, probably in Jerusalem, as van Unnik has recently shown (*Tarsus or Jerusalem; the City of Paul's Youth*), so that he really was a 'Hebrew of the Hebrews'.

The objection based on the omission of reference to the Council of Jerusalem is flimsy: there is no reason why a preacher should state his whole position or refer to all the important issues of the day in every sermon. That the Epistle was not mentioned until *c*. 200 may be due to the fact that it was not of much value for doctrinal polemics. On the positive side it is said that James' speech in Acts 15 resembles the tone and language of the Epistle, and that he appears in Gal. 2.10, as in the Epistle again, a champion of the poor. The absence of Christology or reference to Jesus' example would be natural in his brother. Moreover, the Epistle mentions the issue of faith and works in a manner reminiscent of Paul's Judaistic opponents, without going all the way with them, in the manner of James of Jerusalem. But when all is said, it is little more than to prove that the Epistle *could* have been by James. The fact that the ascription is without qualification might suggest a well-known James for preference, especially so outstanding a figure as the Bishop of Jerusalem, but it may well refer to James the Less or someone else. The name was common enough (Hebrew: Jacob), and the difficulties of the Epistle's excellent, if simple, Greek, the use of Greek form and maxims (5.15), plus its late attestation are not easily set aside. It will be noticed that the estimate of the date above was carried out on the assumption that the writer was not James the Lord's brother and therefore need not necessarily have known Paul's teaching clearly before his letter to the Galatians or even to the Romans.

The Epistle of James, despite its Hellenistic flavour, shows no sympathy at all with the yearnings of the Graeco-Roman world for salvation from time and the flesh, for participation in deep mysteries of God. Not for this writer the soaring Pauline flights of theological thought, we ourselves dead with Christ, risen with him at the right hand of God, our lives hid with him in God, acquitted by faith-union in his Body the Church, members one of another. But (as A. H. McNeile pointed out) in a way James is more profound, for he gets down to the question of the character of God. Paul does not get behind the acts of God to the nature of God; he does not dig down to the foundation on which he builds and so can leave many loose ends which have misled his systematizers. Paul is concerned with what God *does*, James with what he *is*. This is not to say that James is the originator of a new position or has necessarily thought his position out to a consistent conclusion, but he represents a strain of Christian thought which dealt with these matters, and this lends a far greater unity to his work than is sometimes allowed for by those who follow the current fashion of seeing nothing more here than a loosely connected series of conventional moral instructions. It also constitutes the abiding value of James, which is naturally obscured from those who, like Luther, are concerned only with the scheme of salvation or for whom the basic characteristic of God is arbitrary will.

For James, God is pure goodness with no admixture of evil, as also with John (1 Jn 1.5), Plato (*Republic* 3.379ff.), Philo (*De Decal.* 33; *De Fuga* 15; *De Conf. Ling.* 36), and some of the (later) rabbis, e.g. Ḥanina: 'Nothing evil comes from above' (*Gen. Rab.* 51.32c) (see commentary on Jas 1.13–17). It is a fundamental and distinctive position, and that James is not unaware of this is shown by the fact that he warns against other viewpoints (see commentary on 1.14–17). Moreover, in this line of thought the beginning made in the first chapter of Wisdom has been brought to completion and God's invariable and utter goodness is fully harmonized with his creatorhood. It is a great mistake to classify James as a moral tract only. It has a profound theological message with which the Church has never seriously grappled. The whole emphasis of James' teaching on prayer and faith, from the beginning (1.4) to the end (5.13ff.), is for the overcoming of evil and relief from trouble. It is failure to see this which makes some people think it a gloomy epistle.

Directly and consciously from this view stems James' teaching that God is not responsible for temptations in human life, even if these have their function in driving a man back upon God in faith so that they may be overcome. In 1.12–15 he offers a psychological analysis of temptation and sin which also derives from special faith in God's goodness. He is able to slide over from the meaning of *peirasmos* in 1.12 as 'trial' to that of 'temptation' in 1.14, because the doctrine that God sends trial is connected with the notion that he tempts: cf. 'Whom the gods wish to destroy they first make mad', and the Old Testament stories of God inspiring men to evil so that he can vent his wrath on them, e.g. 2 Sam. 24; 1 Kg. 22.18–23; Ezek. 14.9ff.; 2 Th. 2.11f. Calamity and moral evil are connected; and the deterministic Semitic mind (as in the Old Testament) attributes all to God. James discriminates: the calamity is not from God (verse 12) and he is not the author of inward evil (as, e.g., the Qumran doctrine of the two spirits—one good, one evil, but both created by God—would have it). Sin is desire gone bad. In this James is near the rabbinic doctrine of the 'evil inclination', without which men could not live, but is more philosophical and clearminded. The inclination is not evil until it has come to a head in an evil way (1.14f.).

In keeping also with the same interest in God's nature is the teaching that 'the relationships and behaviour of human beings to one another are based on the principle of the dignity of man as man' (McNeile).* God brought him forth with a true word to be a kind of first fruits of his creatures (1.18); he is made in the likeness of God (3.9). And therefore every man is entitled to the opportunity of living the fullest life, not because he is 'in Christ', as Paul would have said (Gal. 3.28; Col. 3.11), but because he is human, made in the image of God. This has, indeed, only been made clear in Christ, and rich and poor are called upon to rejoice in their new-found equality of status (1.9f.). But it is something implicit in their creation. The relation of man to God and man to man in James is something

* 'The love for God that lies behind all brotherly love is also an act of faith' (Stauffer in Kittel, *TWzNT*, s.v. *Agapē*).

that goes down to the roots of things and back to the beginning. In this treatment of the problem of rich and poor the characteristic attitude of Isaiah and Jeremiah and the Psalmists emerges, in which 'poor' practically equals 'righteous', 'holy'. The nature of morality also springs from the character of God. This is why it is important, because it expresses the relationship of man to God, and the nature of the God he worships: *wherefore* let every man be swift to hear . . . slow to wrath, for the wrath of man does not work the righteousness of God (1.19f.; cf. Mt. 5.44f.; Lk. 6.35). The being of man as made in the image of God demands a certain inner nature, and an inward disposition that does not show itself in act does not exist (2.18; cf. 1 Jn 2.4; 3.17; 4.20). This form is filled out with conventional morality derived from the Wisdom school, for which 'wisdom' meant practical righteousness: be careful with your words, keep the peace, beware of anger, do not show favouritism to the rich and flashily dressed.

'What must I do to be saved?' asked the young man; and Jesus answered, 'You know the commandments' (cf. Jas 2.8–11). James would have said the same. He would have agreed with Abraham in the parable, 'If they hear not Moses and the prophets they will not be persuaded though one rose from the dead' (Lk. 16.31). The Law is able to save our souls (1.21) and is a law of liberty (1.25; 2.12).

The Epistle of James is alone among the New Testament epistles in showing a concern for social justice (5.4: 'Behold, the wages of the labourers who mowed your fields, which you kept back by fraud, cry out; and the cries of the harvesters have reached the ears of the Lord of hosts;' cf. also 4.1ff.). Nearest to this comes our Lord's woes upon the rich and his castigation of the religious hypocrites who 'devour widows' houses and for a pretence make long prayers'. The epistle ends with a return to the doctrine of faith, with a section on healing prayer, including confession and forgiveness, in which the forgiveness is an integral part of the healing. This is part and parcel of the teaching upon God's character which is so prominent in the epistle, and of the conviction that the prayer of one who shares that character (the 'righteous man') will be effective.

The Epistle of James has so many characteristic Jewish traits and so few (or ambiguous) references to points of Christian doctrine that some have doubted if it is Christian at all. This difficulty has been exaggerated by inexactitude (cf. on 5.7). James represents an important type of Christianity overshadowed by and misinterpreted through the figure and influence of Paul. Nevertheless the lack of reference to such basic Christian events as the death and resurrection of Christ is remarkable, and it really looks as though the author did not realize the importance of them. The Johannine literature constitutes a bridge between the two types of Christianity, conserving some of the valuable emphases of both.

THE LETTER OF

JAMES

THE LETTER OF
JAMES

1 James, a servant of God and of the Lord Jesus Christ,
To the twelve tribes in the Dispersion: Greeting.
2 Count it all joy, my brethren, when you meet various trials,
3 for you know that the testing of your faith produces steadfastness.

THE SALUTATION 1.1

James: see Introduction.

servant: lit., slave. The phrase 'servant of God' is of Semitic origin, means 'an adherent of God', and is equivalent to 'Christian' when used with 'the Lord Jesus Christ'. There is no reference to the Suffering Servant of 2 Isaiah, for which *pais* and not *doulos* is used. Nor has the phrase much theological significance, though Christians were free from the bondage of sin by becoming slaves of Christ. But the opening is conventional: cf. Rom. 1.1; Phil. 1.1; Tit. 1.1.; etc., and Ac. 4.29. No contrast is intended with Jn 15.15, 'No longer do I call you servants . . . but I have called you friends'.

of God and of the Lord Jesus Christ: this in Greek could mean 'of the God and Lord Jesus Christ', but there is no article, and 'servant of God' looks like a stereotyped phrase: see above.

twelve tribes in the Dispersion: i.e., who are scattered abroad. God's people scattered throughout the world. Most of the great cities of the Roman Empire had their Jewish communities. Here the phrase is probably used of the members of the Christian Church, the new Israel. It has sometimes been thought to indicate Christians who were of Jewish race, and this would cohere with 5.7, where the early and late rains suggest Palestine. Some also think that non-Christian Jews may be included. Cf. Hermas: *Sim.*9.17.1, 'the Twelve Tribes which inhabit the whole world', where the expression may mean 'all the nations (sc. from which the Christian Church is constructed); 1 Pet. 1.1; 2.11, 'strangers and pilgrims'. The notion of the Church as the scattered people of God gained great prominence: Diognetus 5; 2 Clem. 5.1, 5, 6.

The greeting is not necessarily part of the Epistle: the latter looks like an address to a single community, not a general epistle. The confluence of 'greeting' in verse 1 and 'rejoice' in verse 2 which sound similar in Greek (*chairein* and *charan*) may well be accidental, since *chairein* was the conventional greeting. But it was also usual to make puns of this sort: so the Platonic Epistle no. 8 *ad init.*, 'Plato to

the relations and companions of Dion, do well. I shall try to describe the policy
by which you will be most able to "do well" '.

If the greeting is added on (perhaps by the editor who issued James and 1 Peter)
this is no indication of the address of the epistle. But the numerous similarities of
vocabulary in the two epistles plus an editor who attached similar openings is too
complicated to be an acceptable theory.

greeting: lit., rejoicing. A customary salutation in a Greek letter.

THE PLACE OF TRIAL IN THE CHRISTIAN LIFE AND IN
THE PURPOSE OF GOD 1.2–18

TRIAL DRIVES MAN TO THE PRAYER OF FAITH 1.2–8

2. joy: in Greek the word picks up **greeting** in verse 1; see above.
trials: the word for trial (or temptation), *peirasmos*, is used of the eschatological
woes. This may be the meaning in the clause of the Lord's Prayer, 'Lead us not into
temptation'. New prominence has been given to this idea by the frequent occurrence of the notion of 'trial' in the DSS: cf. 1QS 1.17; 8.4; 1QH 2.35; 9.6ff.; 8.26ff.;
11.19ff.; CD 20.27. The language used links up with some of that in James, as
does the background idea of a clear contrast between God's work and the effects
of evil: cf. verses 12ff. But here in James the word 'trials' is plural and the context
indicates that the meaning is that of everyday 'troubles'; not even persecution is
clearly intended. The same word is used by James for both 'trial' (as here) and
'temptation' (verse 14). It has been suggested that early Christian catechisms often
began with a reference to trials: Rom. 5.3; 1 Th. 1.6; Heb. 12.1ff.; 1 Pet. 1.6;
cf. Sir. 2.1ff.
Count it all joy . . . when you meet various trials: only late and doubtful
parallels have been produced from Jewish literature to this attitude of rejoicing
in the face of affliction: the origin is evidently our Lord's own attitude: 'Blessed
are . . .' Mt. 5.10–12; Lk. 6.22f.: cf. Jas 1.12, where the 'Blessed' formula is used in
the same connection, though the reminiscence may be of Dan. 12.12.

3. the testing: preferred also by Weymouth, Goodspeed, and *NEB*. The
meaning could also be, *the genuine element* in your faith (cf. Moffatt). The drift,
then, is not that trials produce steadfastness, but that they provide the opportunity
for steadfastness to have its full effect, to lead to the prayer of faith (verses 4, 5)
and thence to wholeness and completion. The absence of the words 'of your
faith' in some late MSS is not sufficient to count against this. There is a close
parallel to the phrase in 1 Pet. 1.7, and various coincidences with James' language
about steadfastness, testing (the cognate noun, translated in *RSV* 'character') and
boasting (cf. verse 9) appear in Rom. 5.3f. In the latter instance the meaning is that
implied in the test.
faith: it is customary to equate faith with intellectual assent in James, on the
strength of 2.9 (but see the commentary there). James takes faith in a variety of
ways, now as in the Synoptics (1.6), now in the sense of the Christian religion

⁴ And let steadfastness have its full effect, that you may be perfect and complete, lacking in nothing.

⁵ If any of you lacks wisdom, let him ask God, who gives to all men generously and without reproaching, and it will be given him. ⁶ But let him ask in faith, with no doubting, for he who doubts is like a wave of the sea that is driven and tossed by the wind. ⁷, ⁸ For

---

(2.1, 5), now as that aspect of religion that refers to the inner disposition (2.14, cf. 18).

steadfastness: constancy throughout all changes of circumstances, especially endurance under affliction (as Job in Jas 5.11). 'It is, indeed, a characteristic Jewish virtue of all time, and the Christian emphasis on it is a part of the inheritance from Judaism' (Ropes).

4. perfect and complete, lacking in nothing: the meaning of 'perfect' is nearest that in Mt. 5.48; 19.21. In Mk 10.21 Jesus says to the rich man, 'You lack one thing'; in Mt., 'If you would be perfect'. The rich man turns up at Jas 1.10 where the trials of verse 2 have placed him in a position of humiliation, where he can boast of his new (Christian) status. Cf. the Pauline doctrine of faith working itself out in love.

5–8. The resemblance between these verses and Hermas, *Mand.9* is further evidence of the existence of traditional hortatory material.

5. wisdom: the practical righteousness of the Old Testament and Apocrypha, and in particular Proverbs, Sirach and related literature: cf. 2 Chron. 1.10ff.; Wis. 7.7ff.; 8.7; 9.10–18; Prov. 1.2–4; 2 *passim*; Sir. 1.14–20; 51.13–22. This wisdom is the principle of a *perfect and complete* (verse 4) life.

God who gives to all men generously: cf. *Test. Gad.* 7.2, 'God, who gives things good and profitable to all men'.

generously: the adverb cognate with the word for 'single' in Mt. 6.22; Lk. 11.34, there translated in *RSV* 'sound' (but cf. Mt. 20.15 where 'Is thine eye evil? is translated 'Do you begrudge?'). See Rom. 12.8; 2 C. 8.2; 9.11,13; Jos. *Ant.* VII. 13.4 for the noun used to mean 'singleness' or 'generosity'. Simplicity had this meaning for the early Christians (cf. Ac. 2.46).

without reproaching: cf. Odes of Solomon 3.6, 'with the Lord most high and merciful there is no grudging', and Mt. 20.15 quoted above.

Here for the first time the theme of the goodness of God is introduced. Trial drives a man back upon this.

6–8. God is the one **who gives to all men** (verse 5); the complement of this goodness is the **faith** which receives (cf. Mt. 7.7ff.). This must be single-minded, the expression of a whole and complete personality (verse 4). Only so can God's will be done through and for him.

with no doubting: cf. Mk 11.23.

that person must not suppose that a double-minded man, unstable in all his ways, will receive anything from the Lord.

9 Let the lowly brother boast in his exaltation, 10 and the rich in his humiliation, because like the flower of the grass he will pass away. 11 For the sun rises with its scorching heat and withers the grass; its flower falls, and its beauty perishes. So will the rich man fade away in the midst of his pursuits.

12 Blessed is the man who endures trial, for when he has stood the test he will receive the crown of life which God has promised

---

double-minded: cf. *Tanḥ.* 23b, 'If you ask before God you must not have two hearts, one for God and one for something else'; cf. Sir. 1.28. The word used by James is unusual; it occurs also in Hermas, the *Didache,* and also 1 and 2 Clement in the quotation from 'Eldad and Modad' (see the Introduction, p. 12).

unstable: cf. Prov. 28.6 (with mention of rich, cf. the next verses in James); Sir. 2.12f.

9–11. First reference to the contrast between rich and poor, which occurs again at 2.1ff.; 5.1ff.

9. boast in: or, rejoice, glory in.

11. Cf. Isa. 40.6f.; 1 Pet. 1.24. The language is reminiscent of Mk 4.6 and parallels. The thought recurs at Jas 5.14.

CONCLUSION OF THE FIRST SECTION 1.12

Blessed is the man who endures trial: the sentiment of 1.2 is repeated in beatitude form (cf. Mt. 5.10–12; Ps. 1.1); but the words may be an echo of Dan. 12.12.

the crown of life: 1QS 4.7f. promises for 'the sons of truth' among other things 'eternal rejoicing in the victorious life of eternity, and a crown of glory' (Brownlee's translation). The imagery is similar to Wis. 5.16ff.; 18.24. In the latter place Moses is thus described: 'thy majesty was upon the diadem of his head', i.e., his face had the afterglow of the Shekinah (cf. Exod. 34.33ff.; 2 C. 3.13ff.). In the Odes of Solomon (1 *passim*; 5.12; 9.8f.; 17.1f.; 20.7f.) the crown is the living Lord himself, or his grace. Cf. also 2 Tim. 2.5; 4.8; 1 Pet. 5.4 and Heb. 2.9.

which God has promised: the word 'God' is not represented in the original, which simply has 'which he has promised'. Late authorities insert 'the Lord'. There may be a reference to a lost saying of Jesus: cf. Rev. 2.10, where the first and last and living one says to the church in Smyrna, 'Be faithful to death and I will give you the crown of life'. (But see S–B *in loc.* for the Jewish habit of leaving out God's name as subject.)

to those who love him. ¹³ Let no one say when he is tempted, "I am tempted by God"; for God cannot be tempted with evil and he himself tempts no one; ¹⁴ but each person is tempted when he is lured and enticed by his own desire. ¹⁵ Then desire when it has

---

those who love him: cf. Jas 2.5—probably a technical term for the righteous in the future world. Box (*Test. Abr.* xxiii) quotes Simeon ben Joḥai (*Sifre Dt.* 10a) on the 'seven classes of righteous ones who will see God's majesty in the world to come'. The first are 'those who love him', who are like the sun: cf. the Targum on Jg. 5.31, 'But let them that love him be as the sun when he goeth forth in his might', and with this, Mt. 13.43. Cf. also Exod. 20.6.

GOD'S INNOCENCE 1.13–18

James comes to the basis of his teaching in the character of God, which is invariable goodness (verse 17). He takes his stand on the principle enunciated in 3.11f.: 'Does a spring pour forth from the same opening fresh water and brackish? Can a fig tree, my brethren, yield olives, or a grapevine figs? No more can salt water yield fresh.' The man who endures trial as a Christian knows that he is on the side of God in confronting it.

13. Let no one say when he is tempted, 'I am tempted by God': i.e., 'Let no one when he is tried say, "I am being tested by God"'. The word 'tempt' can refer to outward troubles or inward solicitations to evil. Jesus tells his disciples in Gethsemane to pray in order that they may not enter into temptation (Mk 14.38); the petition in the Lord's prayer implies the same idea.

God cannot be tempted with evil could mean 'cannot tempt to evil' if this idea were not expressed in the next clause: the idea is that God has nothing to do with temptation at all, either in the sense of seducing people or sending trials upon them. This is the line of New Testament teaching which appears also in the Fourth Gospel (Sidebottom: *The Christ of the Fourth Gospel*, pp. 54, 158f., 173, 205) and has its roots in the Wisdom literature, particularly the Wisdom of Solomon. See on verses 14–17 below.

14. lured and enticed by his own desire: James concentrates on moral temptation, which comes from within: cf. Sir. 15.11–20, beginning, 'Say not, It is through the Lord that I fell away'. Parallels have been drawn with the DSS doctrine of the two spirits, and this in turn has been traced to Iranian influence. But James is, in fact, nearer to classical Iranian teaching as also to that of Plato, for he also holds that God is not responsible for evil. In the DSS the two spirits are both created by God, although they represent the antitheses of good and evil; and it is not inconceivable that James is here opposing some such doctrine. The two spirits occur in *The Testaments of the Twelve Patriarchs*, but there they are nearer to the rabbinic two inclinations. It is to be noted, however, that the evil inclination (*yēṣer hārā'*)

conceived gives birth to sin; and sin when it is full-grown brings forth death.

16 Do not be deceived, my beloved brethren. ¹⁷ Every good endowment and every perfect gift is from above, coming down from the Father of lights with whom there is no variation or shadow

---

is rather the soil from which evil springs than evil in itself, and is indeed an integral part of human nature, necessary for such activities as procreation and business.

desire: always with pejorative significance in the New Testament, except at Lk. 22.15; Phil. 1.23; 1 Th. 2.17; Rev. 18.14. Here it is on the way to being wrong.

15. brings forth death: cf. Wis. 1.12ff., beginning 'Do not invite death by the error of your life, nor bring on destruction by the works of your hands'. See below on verse 17. The whole passage urges that death and destruction do not originate with God.

16. Do not be deceived: James delivers a warning against those who teach that evil can come from God. The form of the warning suggests that the converse is intended, namely that good cannot come from anywhere else. Both aspects of the matter are true, but the former more likely to be questioned.

17. Every good endowment and every perfect gift: the rendering is infelicitous, since the word translated 'endowment' is the commoner. It appears often in Sirach, e.g., 11.17; 18.15ff.; 20.14; 26.14; 32.11, but James would not have agreed with the sentiment expressed in 11.17. In *Test. Zeb.* 1.3 a 'good gift' is Zebulun's description of his own birth. Any ordinary blessing is therefore intended. The phrase makes a hexameter in Greek, which may be accidental; but it may also be a quotation from some unknown source.

is from above: that only good comes from God was a widespread Jewish doctrine, especially in Alexandrine circles. Philo reiterates it, e.g., *De Decal.* 33; *De Fuga* 15; *De Conf. Ling.* 36. The last will serve to illustrate: 'God is the cause only of good things, and of nothing that is bad, since he is himself the most ancient of beings and the most perfect goodness.' This is practically a quotation from Plato, *Republic* 3.379ff. Wisdom 1.14 combines the reflection with belief in God's creatorhood: 'He created all things that they might have their being, and the generative powers of the world are healthful; and there is no poison of destruction in them . . . but ungodly men by their works and words called it to them. . . .' The whole passage should be compared, and with it also Jas 1.15. The notion underlying the Greek view appealed to some of the (later) rabbis: cf. Gen. Rab. 51.32c, R. Ḥanina said, 'Nothing evil comes from above' (S–B, *in loc.*). But cf. Jas 4.12. See also on 3.15.

the Father of lights: 'lights' has often been thought to refer to celestial bodies, i.e., stars and planets; 'no variation or shadow due to change' in the next verse might then be an eclipse, and verse 18 could be taken to refer to creation by

due to change. ¹⁸ Of his own will he brought us forth by the word of truth that we should be a kind of first fruits of his creatures.

19 Know this, my beloved brethren. Let every man be quick to hear, slow to speak, slow to anger, ²⁰ for the anger of man does not work the righteousness of God. ²¹ Therefore put away all filthiness

---

emanation with God as the Father of the universe in the Philonic sense. Reference can also be made to 1QS 3.20 where 'rule over the sons of righteousness is in the hand of the Prince of Lights'. In *Test. Abr.* B 7 the sun is called 'father of the light', but the same phrase is used in *Apoc. Mos.* 46 apparently for the uncreated light.

with whom is no variation or shadow due to change: various emendations of the text have been suggested, but the meaning is not affected. God is the pure light without changing clouds passing over the face of the sun and so causing shadows. Here is a connection with 1 Jn 1.5, where the doctrine expressed in James is presented as the sum of the Gospel: 'This is the message we have heard from him and proclaim to you, that God is light and in him is no darkness at all.'

JAMES TURNS TO THE ETHICAL IMPLICATIONS OF THE TEACHING UPON GOD 1.18–21

The status of the Christian requires appropriate behaviour, cf. 1 Pet. 1.22f. Far from working for our destruction, God has bestowed the highest honour upon us.
18. Of his own will: i.e., deliberately.

he brought us forth: only rarely in the New Testament is it possible to find a direct reference to the notion that men are the offspring of God rather than his creatures: e.g., Ac. 17.28. This would not in any case be what is implied in that interpretation of verse 17 which makes God father of the universe, for men are here separated from the rest of creation as its 'first fruits'. It would, however, fit in with the Hermetic teaching of *Poimandres* that 'the Father of All, the Nous being life and light, brought forth a Man equal to himself, whom he loved as his own child' (*CH* 1.12). Philo, too, regards the ideal counterpart of man as an offspring and not a creature of God (*Leg. All.* 1.31). The language of James is close enough to suggest some acquaintance with this type of thought, though there is no reference here to the ideal Man. (When in *CH* 1.9 God 'brings forth *with a word*' the demiurge, Dodd thinks the italicized expression may have been inserted from this verse of James.) In 1 Pet. 1.3 the Resurrection is the cause of the new birth, and this the early Church thought of as a new creation; but James does not mention it.

by the word of truth: lit., by a word of truth, i.e., a true word. This could mean (1) the Gospel, (2) the Law, or (3) the original creative word of God. (1) seems unlikely without the article: cf. 2 C. 6.7 where the meaning is quite indeterminate;

and we should expect 'men' not 'creatures'. The parallel passage in 1 Pet. 1.23 defines the expression 'word' as the Gospel in a way which suggests that the writer is quoting from a tradition in which it was not so defined, not only in respect of the Isaiah 40.6ff. quotation but also in verse 23; see on verse 21 below. (2) 'a word of truth' seems to describe the Law in *Test. Gad* 3.1, and Philo calls Israel 'first-fruits' (*De Spec. Leg.* 4; cf. Jer. 2.3); but there is no parallel to God giving birth to Israel by means of the Law. (3) In *Poimandres* (see above) a 'holy word' comes uṗ.. the chaos to effect creation, and the meaning is the voice of God as in Genesis. The reference to 'creatures' shows that creation is in view.

first fruits: not necessarily in the sense of first in time; quality can also be intended. Philo speaks of Israel as first among peoples in this sense. Adam was the *primus* among creatures, having dominion over the others.

of his creatures: a word used often in the Wisdom literature. The consensus of modern opinion is that the passage refers to Christian regeneration, but there is nothing in the context to lead up to this, unless we assume that James is a baptismal exhortation. This is not impossible, and there is no reason why a writer should not suddenly burst out in praise of what has happened to him as a Christian. If this is the case, then the new birth is being thought of in terms of the original creation. Or the original creation itself may be intended in the way it was regarded by Hellenistic Jewish thinkers, a view which has the authority of Hort. It seems the more probable as following more naturally from the context: 'brought us forth . . . a kind of first fruits of his creatures' (but cf. Rom. 8.21); the same idea recurs in 3.9, where God is called 'the Lord and Father' in immediate connection with 'made in the image of God'.

EXHORTATION TO DEEDS IN CONFORMITY WITH THIS DOCTRINE OF GOD 19–27

19. Quick to hear, slow to speak, slow to anger: conventional Jewish exhortation: cf. Ec. 7.9; Sir. 5.11; also Mt. 5.22; Eph. 4.26.

20. the anger of man does not work the righteousness of God: whether this means 'the anger of man does not constitute right dealing in the sight of God' or 'the anger of man does not produce the righteousness that is of God', the word 'righteousness' in Jewish thought has not necessarily the sense of uprightness or strict piety. It embraces also the 'goodness' which we know of in God in the sense of beneficence and benevolence. Coming so closely after the enunciation of the doctrine of God's invariable goodness, the word must have this meaning here. God's goodness is not shown in the anger of man (cf. Mt. 6.9; 5.16 for the typically Jewish idea of the action of man showing forth the character of his God). The contrast is not between the anger of man and the wrath of God (which does not figure in James), but between man's anger and God's goodness. Hence human anger is altogether condemned (cf. Mt. 5.22ff.) and warned against as not contributing to the vindication of the divine righteousness.

21. Put away: Selwyn held that traces of the 'Christian holiness code' discerned

and rank growth of wickedness and receive with meekness the implanted word, which is able to save your souls.

22 But be doers of the word, and not hearers only, deceiving yourselves. 23 For if any one is a hearer of the word and not a doer,

---

by Carrington behind 1 and 2 Thessalonians received an amplification later in the form that appears in 1 Peter and James. The earlier form, designed to preserve the Church as a 'neo-Levitical community, at once sacerdotal and sacrificial', was probably the first draft of a baptismal catechism, 'and seems to have had specially in mind the elementary needs of Gentile Christians, and the fears of Jewish Christians, as these were made clear at the Council of Jerusalem' (*The First Epistle of Peter*, pp. 459f.). The later form began with the idea of 'the word of truth' (cf. Jas 1.18) and substituted for the earlier exhortations to 'avoid' the injunction to 'lay aside' evil (as here and at 1 Pet. 2.1; cf. Eph. 4.25, 31; Col. 3.8; the word is common in Greek writers for the renunciation of immoral behaviour). This is a speculative theory imposed on this particular epistle by comparison with others (see Introduction above, p. 3). It assumes (as we have seen reason to doubt) that verse 18 refers to baptism.

wickedness (*kakia*): the meaning is the general one of depravity, vice; but the word often has the meaning of 'malice'. Connected with **'filthiness'**, however, it probably means the former, which does not seem to agree with Col. 3.8; 1 Pet. 2.1 where the meaning is 'malice'. Thus James, once more, does not fit easily into the catechism pattern.

rank growth: 'the phrase calls attention to the fact that wickedness is in reality an excrescence on character, not a normal part of it.' So Ropes, from whose note and references to Philo on pruning the *RSV* translation probably derives. The word means literally 'surplus'. But the reference may be to the Christian teaching of 'putting off the old man' and 'putting on the new' which probably antecedes Paul (Eph. 4.22, 24).

meekness: i.e., without **anger**; gentleness, humility, courtesy, considerateness.

implanted word: the word translated by 'implanted' means inborn, natural, and recalls the Stoic *logos endiathetos* which also appears in Philo as opposed to the *logos prophorikos*. It means 'thought' and is used of the reason immanent in the world. The phrase *endiathetos anthrōpos* occurs in *CH* 13.7, for the 'inner man'. In Wis. 12.10 evil (*kakia*) is said to be 'implanted' (innate) in the original inhabitants of Canaan. The *Epistle of Barnabas* 1.2 speaks of how 'deeply rooted within is the grace of the spiritual gift you have received'. Thus the word can be used not only of something natural but also of a bestowed gift. But the idea is still difficult with the word 'receive'; there is little to be said for the translation, 'receive the word which will become innate in you' which we tend to presuppose in reading the text. Later (verses 22ff.) this 'word' appears to be identified with 'the law of liberty';

James thus may have been thinking of this law in a double sense as that which answers to the deliveries of conscience and is identical with them: cf. Rom 2.14, 'When Gentiles who have not the law do by nature what the law requires, they are a law to themselves, even though they do not have the law'.

If the 'word' here is connected in the author's mind with that 'word of truth' which brought forth men (verse 18), and with the notion (in this verse) of putting off the old man and putting on the new, there may be a distant reference to that Name of God by which creation was effected (Sidebottom, *The Christ of the Fourth Gospel*, pp. 38-47) and which expresses itself through it: cf. Odes of Solomon 41.15, 'The Messiah is truly one; and he was known before the foundation of the world, That he might save souls for ever by the truth of his name'; and also **save your souls** here in James. But, if so, it is not in the forefront of the author's mind and may belong to the source he seems to share with 1 Peter. The parallel passage there reads, 'You have been born anew, not of perishable seed but of imperishable, through the living and abiding word of God' (1 Pet. 1.23) but the imagery reflects Johannine language (1 Jn 2.14, 'word abiding'; 1 Jn 3.9, *RSV* 'nature'='seed'; Jn 3.3, 'born anew') cf. on verse 18 above. The Peshitta Syriac translation 'word that is planted in our nature' recalls Lk. 8.11, 'The seed is the word of God,' etc. The next verse reads, 'The ones along the path are those who have heard; then the devil comes and takes away the word from their hearts, that they may not believe and be saved': cf. this and the next verse in James, '. . . implanted word, which is able to save your souls. But be doers of the word, and not hearers only . . .' Paul also in Rom. 2.23 uses this language in the place where he is speaking of the Gentiles obeying the law in their own consciences (Rom. 2.13ff.).

able to save your souls: the same phrase is used of 'the commandments' which are 'beautiful and joyful and glorious' in Hermas, *Sim.* VI.1.1. If 'word' thus= 'commandment', this is the first statement of James' position that works can save. The transition from the creative word of verse 18 to word as 'commandment' and 'Gospel' (the two notions coalesce: see on verse 25) would be easy for a Jew who thought of the law as the 'blueprint' of creation as well as the moral life.

DOERS, NOT HEARERS ONLY 1.22-2.26

22. doers of the word: a Hebraism for 'those who obey the commandment'. **Doers** appears three times in James (all in this chapter—1.22, 23, 25), and elsewhere in the New Testament only in Rom. 2.13 (see above on verse 21). Cf. Mt. 7.21, 26; 21.28ff.; Lk. 11.28; 12.47.

deceiving yourselves: by thinking that hearing alone is enough.

23. A man looking in a mirror sees his natural face; the one who looks into the **perfect law of liberty** (verse 25) sees his ideal self, the self he ought to be. The words for 'natural face' are, literally 'face of his genesis': the context of verses 18 and 21 may imply a reference to the creation hymn where man is created in the image of God. In the law of liberty he sees his true image (Nairne).

he is like a man who observes his natural face in a mirror; ²⁴ for he observes himself and goes away and at once forgets what he was like. ²⁵ But he who looks into the perfect law, the law of liberty, and perseveres, being no hearer that forgets but a doer that acts, he shall be blessed in his doing.

26 If any one thinks he is religious, and does not bridle his tongue but deceives his heart, this man's religion is vain. ²⁷ Religion that is

---

24. he goes away: the perfect is used in the Greek: he 'is gone off' and so forgets. Out of sight, out of mind.

25. the perfect law, the law of liberty: apparently the 'word' of verse 21. Both epithets could have been used by a loyal Jew of the Torah. It was the supreme gift of God to man, comparable with the gift of the Gospel as this appeared to Christians: Ps. 19.7 'The Law of the Lord is perfect, reviving the soul' (Heb.). 1QH 4.6; 18.29 speaks of perfect light (lit., light of perfection) in connection with the Covenant and Torah. The keeping of it led to freedom: Philo (*Vit. Mos.* 2.9) said it was not for slaves like those laws which were imposed, but for free men (cf. Ps. 40.8; 1.2; 119.97, 45). *Aboth* 6.2 says, 'No man is free but he who labours in the Torah'. Dodd's parallels from Greek writings (*The Bible and the Greeks*, p. 40) are (contrary to what he avers) no closer, if as close. The argument that Ps. 19.7 was not available to James because he only used the LXX is really without force; the Hebraic Psalms were in existence, and in principle the ideas contained in them were as accessible as those in the DSS and more so than those in the rabbis. James' phrase is used by Irenaeus of 'God's word': see on 4.1.

For the designation of Christianity as a law, see 1 C. 9.21; Rom. 3.27; Gal. 6.2; Jn 13.34; 1 Jn 2.7f; 1 Tim. 1.7 and cf. Dodd, *Gospel and Law*, pp. 64ff. for a re-examination of the notion that Christ put an end to all law. In Hermas, Barnabas, Justin Martyr and Irenaeus the conception of Christianity as a law is prominent, but the idea may need revision that this is a declension from the 'Pauline' position, for this never seems to have held the whole field. It is, in fact, doubtful whether the current rigid distinction between Gospel and Law can hold; the special ethical teaching of Jesus is part of the new life: cf. the discussion in Jeremias, *The Sermon on the Mount*, in the course of which he holds that Jesus' ethical teaching is part of the Gospel and that Dodd's definition of *didachē* as ethical teaching is too narrow.

26. religious, religion: the adjective is extremely rare. The reference is mainly to the outward aspect of worship, public observance. Without morality and service (verses 26f.) this is empty (**vain**) like idolatry (cf. Jer. 2.5; 10.3; and Ac. 14.15; 1 Pet. 1.18).

27. pure and undefiled: fulfilling the requirements of true worship, as did

pure and undefiled before God and the Father is this: to visit orphans and widows in their affliction, and to keep oneself unstained from the world.

2 My brethren, show no partiality as you hold the faith of our Lord Jesus Christ, the Lord of glory. ² For if a man with gold

---

ritual purity for ancient peoples, not least the Pharisees of James' day. But it is 'the world' that stains (see below).

before God: the equivalent of the Hebrew expression signifying 'in the sight or presence of God'; cf. the similar idea in Lk. 16.15. For the teaching that religious observance takes second place to humanity, see Mt. 5.23ff.; 9.13; 12.7; 23.33; 25.35f.; Mk 12.40.

God and the Father: lit., 'the God and Father': cf. Paul's formulas 'the God and Father of our Lord Jesus Christ' and so on for the 'new' God of the Christians.

The emphasis on practical good works is typically Jewish (cf. Mic. 6.8).

affliction: bereavement.

world: life as organized without reference to God, on the basis of greed, power, artifice, and omnicompetence. The usage is most prominent in the Gospel and Epistles of John. The terminology is curiously absent from pre-Christian literature. In the rabbis God created 'the world' but 'this world' is opposed to 'the world to come'. In *CH* 6.4 the world is 'the fulness of evil' and the language of this verse in James is reminiscent of Hermetism, with the important exception of the definition of religion in terms of good works (Dodd, *The Bible and the Greeks*, p. 14). 1 Enoch 48.7 has, 'Because they have hated and despised this world of unrighteousness'. *Lev. Rab.* 26 calls this world a 'world of untruth'. *Test. Iss.* 4.6 comes nearest with 'Shunning eyes (made) evil through the error of *the world*'. For the likeness to Johannine thought, cf. on Jas 4.4.

The virtue inculcated by James has nothing to do with a primness which will not seek contact with a soiled world, but excludes a piety which is complacent with involvement in it.

Partiality. Chapter 2 continues the emphasis upon deeds as against formal religious observance. The diatribe style is indicated in the rhetorical questions and the introduction of the imaginary interlocutor: see verses 2ff., 14ff., 18ff.

2.1. partiality: favouritism, lit., 'face-taking', a noun formed from the Semitic idiom, in which the word 'face' stands (as often) for 'person': God is no 'respecter of persons' (Ac. 10.34) and even his enemies could not accuse Jesus of it (Mk 12.14)! His followers must be the same. But the Greek suggests that they had not been: 'Stop showing partiality.'

hold the faith: a Greek usage. For **faith** see on 1.3.

of our Lord Jesus Christ: cf. Mk 11.22, lit. 'Have the faith of God'; i.e., the

4

rings and in fine clothing comes into your assembly, and a poor
man in shabby clothing also comes in, ³ and you pay attention to the
one who wears the fine clothing and say, 'Have a seat here, please,'
while you say to the poor man, 'Stand there,' or, 'Sit at my feet,'

---

genitive is objective: it is faith *in* Jesus, not the faith Jesus held, though Hort's
paraphrase 'that comes from him and depends on him' is not entirely superfluous,
for faith in Christ involves faith in what he stands for.

the Lord of glory: 'the Lord' is not represented in the original, being inserted
by the translators. The choice therefore is between 'the faith of our Lord Jesus
Christ of glory', which could be taken as a Hebraism for 'our glorious Lord Jesus
Christ' (cf. 1 C. 2.8; Ps. 29.3; Ac. 7.2; Eph. 1.17), and 'the faith of our Lord Jesus
Christ the Glory' (Bengel, Hort, etc.). Mayor suggested that this meant that
Jesus was being identified with the Shekinah, the cloud of glory, the dwelling
of God with men (cf. Exod. 33.7–23). This is not impossible, for the Shekinah
is a technical term which was widely known and has left traces on the New Testament: cf. Jn 1.14 'tabernacled'; Mk 9.7 (Lk. 9.34; esp. Mt. 17.5; cf. 2 Pet. 1.17);
Lk. 2.9; Ac. 7.55; 2 C. 3 and 4 *passim*. In 1 C. 11.7 man is the glory of God,
and Christ is the brightness of God's glory in Heb. 1.3, where the reference is
to Wis. 7.25f.

2ff. Doubtless a hypothetical case, yet surely not entirely divorced from local
conditions. The picture of the assembly or synagogue with the rich man in splendid
clothes and the poor man in filthy rags is a vivid reminder of the state of affairs in
Palestine: cf. Lk. 16.19ff.

2. assembly: lit., synagogue. The use of the word is no sign by itself of an
early date for James. Christian Palestinian Aramaic used a word for both 'synagogue' and 'church' which is related to the Hebrew word for synagogue.*
shabby: filthy (the cognate noun is used in 1.21), contrasting with 'fine', lit.,
bright, shining. The reference may be either to 'clean' or 'splendid' clothing. The
man in vile clothes is still a brother.

3. pay attention: take an interest in, look after, attend to.
'Have a seat here' . . . **'Stand there.'** Emphatic pronouns are introduced in the
Greek: 'You sit here' . . . 'You stand there.'
please: lit., 'you will do well', the usual way of saying 'please' in the papyri.
But the versions (Syriac, Latin, Ethiopic) have 'well' and this fits the context: i.e.,
'in a good place' (*AV*). Cf. 2 Pet. 1.19, where the same expression is rendered by
the *RSV* 'You will do well'.

There is little to commend the view that James is here referring to the precept

---

* When Gaster, *The Scriptures of the Dead Sea Sect*, pp. 25f., says that the 'early
Palestinian Christians' used the Syriac counterpart of the Hebrew word 'ēḏāh for
'the Church' he is evidently thinking of the Peshitta version only.

⁴ have you not made distinctions among yourselves, and become judges with evil thoughts? ⁵ Listen, my beloved brethren. Has not God chosen those who are poor in the world to be rich in faith and

---

in 1QS that all members of the community are to be graded by intelligence and character alone.

4. have you not made distinctions among yourselves: the word translated 'made distinctions' means 'doubt' in 1.6 (cf. Mt. 21.21). This is a sense confined to the New Testament, where the meanings 'hesitate, waver' also occur. The meaning would then be that the addressees of the epistle were not holding fast to their profession by showing partiality. Beyschlag connected the notion of 'doubt' with the double-minded man in 1.16 and suggested that those who showed favouritism were in this category, the opposite of 'faith'. But this is to fail in discrimination between two senses of the word 'faith'. 'You do not decide in your own minds' (*sc.* about the true position of Christians in the matter) is another possible rendering which produces the same general meaning. Yet another is 'Are you not divided in your minds (or, among yourselves)'. The *NEB* has 'You are inconsistent'.

yourselves: lit., 'in yourselves'.

The two clauses of the verse, divided by 'and', appear to be parallel: 'made distinctions'='being judges'; 'in yourselves'='with . . . thoughts'.

judges with evil thoughts: i.e.. unworthy opinions or motives. The entire verse might read, 'Do you not discriminate in your own minds and (thus) become unworthy judges?' The word 'judges' owes its introduction to the notion of judgment implicit in discrimination, and the further thought suggests itself to the writer that in fact the 'partiality' (verse 1) he speaks of is the characteristic of *bad* judges, so he adds 'with evil thoughts'.

5. chosen: God chooses people in the Old Testament: Israel in Dt. 4.37; 7.7., etc.; the Servant in Isa. 42.1. In the New Testament see, e.g., Lk. 9.35 and parallels, cf. Mk 1.11 and parallels; Jn 15.16, and, especially for this passage, 1 C. 1.26ff.: 'For consider your call, brethren: not many of you were wise according to worldly standards, not many were powerful, not many were of noble birth . . . God chose what is low and despised in the world . . .' Paul articulates the thought into his theology of justification of the ungodly and of the paradoxical appearance of the power and wisdom of God in a world mad with power and dazzled by riches and status (1 C 1.25), but the sentiment and even the phraseology are evidently earlier. James echoes both. He may be thinking of God's choice of the poor as being in his mind from all eternity (Eph. 1.3f.; 1 Pet. 1.1f.). See S–B i.974; ii.335; iii.579f. for the Jewish belief in the pre-mundane election of Israel.

poor: 'the poor' or humble in the land, always in Israel regarded as the object of God's special concern, are in the post-exilic psalms, second Isaiah and Jeremiah

heirs of the kingdom which he has promised to those who love him? ⁶ But you have dishonoured the poor man. Is it not the rich who oppress you, is it not they who drag you into court? ⁷ Is it not they who blaspheme that honourable name by which you are called?

8 If you really fulfil the royal law, according to the scripture,

---

practically identified with the holy, pious or godly. At Qumran voluntary poverty on a monastic basis was the rule. The early Church at Jerusalem seems to have practised a primitive communism. The sect of Ebionites, who rejected the divinity of Christ and kept the Jewish law, may have derived their name from the adjective 'ebyōn, poor; and this form of Christianity has reminded many of James, with his Jewishness and lack of interest in the person of Christ. It certainly may have grown out of the beliefs of such a group at Jerusalem; and the existence of Wisdom-influence in James is no objection to his association with it. The DSS show strong Wisdom influence, and it is generally agreed now that Palestinian Judaism was more affected by Hellenism than was formerly believed. That Paul, however, could write almost the same thing to Corinth warns against the assumption of a doctrinaire distinction 'poor-rich' in James. He certainly felt riches and rich men to be hostile, but he speaks of 'poor people' rather than 'the poor man', as he does 'righteous people' rather than 'the righteous one'. Most of the early Christians were poor; in the community to which James wrote one or two rich men showed interest. (If this had not been the case there would have been small reason to mention them.) The result is to wean some of the others from the pure milk of their faith.

in the world: lit., 'to the world', i.e., in the world's eyes. For the same phrase, cf. Ac. 7.20, 'beautiful before God' (lit. 'to God'). For 'world' in James see on 1.27 and 4.4. C. F. D. Moule suggests a contrast with Mt. 5.3, 'poor in the religious sense', so here, 'literally poor'.

rich in faith: Lk. 12.21, 'So is he who lays up treasure for himself, and is not rich toward God', i.e., in the sight of God.

heirs of the kingdom: cf. Mt. 5.3, 5, 'Blessed are the poor in spirit, for theirs is the kingdom of heaven . . . Blessed are the meek, for they shall inherit the earth'. When the word 'kingdom' is used without qualification in Jewish literature, it refers to the secular authority: e.g. *Aboth* 3.2: R. Ḥanina, the deputy high-priest, said, 'Pray for the welfare of the government (kingdom), since but for the fear of it men would swallow each other alive' (cf. Ac. 1.6). In one strain of synoptic teaching, Jesus is represented as promising the 'kingdom' to his disciples, without qualification: Lk. 12.32, 'The Father has chosen to give you the kingdom'; Lk. 22.29, 'I appoint to you a kingdom'; cf. Rev. 1.6 and the curious expression 'the tribulation and the kingdom and the patient endurance' in Rev. 1.9; also Heb. 12.28. Matthew is specially prone to use the word 'kingdom' by itself:

Mt. 4.23; 13.19, 38; 24.14 and 25.34, 'inherit the kingdom prepared for you from the foundation of the world'. It is with this latter strain that James shows closest affinity. Cf. also Jn 3.3, 5 with Wis. 10.10, where the kingdom of God appears to refer to the blessed world 'above'. To inherit the kingdom is equivalent to inheriting 'eternal life': Mt. 19.29; Mk 10.17; Lk. 10.25; 18.18. Despite various attempts, it is not possible to define 'kingdom of God' as it is used in the Gospels or outside closer than to say it stands for the sum total of blessing bestowed by God in Christ and consisting in the highest life in which we are yet truly at home. It is in this sense that James uses the elliptical expression 'kingdom'.

promised: Dalman derives the New Testament conception of the 'promise' from the rabbinic phrase 'be assured that one is a son of the age to come' or 'will inherit the age to come' (*Keth.* 111a; *Sifre Dt.* 305; Targ. Ruth 2.13). The idea originally goes back to the promises to Abraham (Gen. 22.17) and of a land flowing with milk and honey (Exod. 3.8), both of which texts were used by the early Church of the Christian heritage. In 1 Jn 2.25 the promise is of eternal life, cf. 1 Tim. 4.8: 'godliness . . . holds promise for the present life and also for the life to come'.

those who love him: cf. 1.12 and the note there. The phrase seems to confirm that the kingdom=the 'world to come' or the 'world above'.

6. Further reflection of the conditions of the addressees. They are evidently expected to understand their position as a downtrodden class. This is, in fact, the strongest attack of this kind in the New Testament.

drag you into court: not necessarily religious persecution, but the possibility is open; cf. verse 7. The ruling classes were those who dragged the Christians into court: Mk 13.9. For other possible oppressions, see 5.4, 6.

7. they who blaspheme: this seems to refer to non-Christians. The notion of the name of God being profaned by Christians who are a bad advertisement for their faith (cf. on 1.20), which reflects the usage of Ezekiel (e.g., 36.23) and occurs in Rom. 2.24 (Isa. 52.5), is not in question. But a *class* is being spoken of; there is nothing to rule out the idea that the 'man with gold rings and fine clothing' of verse 2 could be an adherent. See 1 Enoch 94.8f., etc. for the blasphemy of the rich among the Jews, where the blasphemy consists in trusting in riches and forgetting God.

honourable name: in 1QS 6.27 the name of God is called 'the honoured Name'. In the rabbis the 'special Name' (*šēm hammᵉyuḥāḏ*) means 'the divine name written in full', i.e., God himself: cf. Dt. 16.2, etc. Here it is the name of Christ (cf. 1 Pet. 4.14ff.). With the whole expression 'the honourable name by which you are called', cf. 2 Mac. 8.15; Hermas, *Sim.* VIII.6.4. It is the occurrence of these words in James which lends plausibility to the idea that rich men who are Christians are in question, cf. the Ezekiel passage mentioned above.

MORALITY IS ONE AND INDIVISIBLE 2.8–26

8. the royal law: the expression is difficult to parallel from Jewish sources.

'You shall love your neighbour as yourself,' you do well. ⁹ But if you show partiality, you commit sin, and are convicted by the law as transgressors. ¹⁰ For whoever keeps the whole law but fails in one point has become guilty of all of it. ¹¹ For he who said, 'Do not commit adultery,' said also, 'Do not kill.' If you do not commit adultery but do kill, you have become a transgressor of the law. ¹² So speak and so act as those who are to be judged under the law of liberty. ¹³ For judgment is without mercy to one who has shown no mercy; yet mercy triumphs over judgment.

A similar one occurs in Ps-Plato, *Minos* 317C, 'the righteous law is the royal law'. In *Ep.* 8.354C the expression is 'the Law became supreme king of men' and later 'kingly laws' are mentioned. The meaning oscillates between 'law worthy of a king' and 'law that is itself king'; if the former sense is accepted it could be understood by a Jew as referring to 'the law of God'. But cf. 4 Mac. 14.2 for piety described as 'royal' and 'free' (cf. Jas 2.13). Here the context shows that the Jewish law is intended, in its moral aspect.

Sayings of the rabbis can be quoted to the effect that 'love your neighbour' is the highest principle of the Law (cf. Mk 12.31). But it seems unlikely that 'law' (*nomos*) should be used in the sense of 'commandment' (*entolē*). It is possible, however, that this commandment is taken as the fulfilling of the law (Rom. 13.8ff.): 'If you fulfil the law in accordance with the scripture "You shall love, etc." you do well'. There is no contradiction on this showing with the following; the 'royal law' is not just part of the law, it is *the impartiality* which is taken as part of the whole (2.9ff.). The connection with the preceding then is 'If you really want to fulfil the royal law which is summed up in "Love your neighbour" (cf. Gal. 6.2), you must obey the rule of impartiality—among others'.

according to the scripture: i.e., Lev. 19.18.

9. you are convicted by the law: as laid down in Lev. 19.15.

10. Cf. Gal. 5.3; 3.10; Mt. 5.19. Once more James shows affinity with Matthew's special material. Various comparable rabbinic opinions are adduced by the commentators, e.g., 'Whoever is guilty on account of one (commandment) is guilty of the rest'.

guilty: the word (*enochos*) occurs also in Mt. 5.21ff. and Mk 14.64; Mt. 26.66 (at Jesus' condemnation), among other places in the New Testament. It is especially appropriate here, as representing the technical Hebrew term *ḥayyāḇ*.

12. to be judged: James' stress is on the final judgment; Paul's on interim justification: verse 12 leads naturally to the argument in verses 14ff. which appears to clash with Paul's teaching.

law of liberty: see on 1.25.

14 What does it profit, my brethren, if a man says he has faith but has not works? Can his faith save him? ¹⁵ If a brother or sister is ill-clad and in lack of daily food, ¹⁶ and one of you says to them, 'Go in peace, be warmed and filled,' without giving them the

---

13. judgment is without mercy to one who has shown no mercy: the notion is common in Jewish teaching: Sir. 28.2f.; *Test. Zeb.* 5 and 8; *Meg.* 28b, etc. (cf. Mt. 5.7; 6.14; 7.1, etc.). The converse appears in *p Bab.Ķ* .6c: 'When you are merciful, God is merciful to you', Sanh. 51b: 'One in heaven is merciful to him who shows mercy to creatures'.

mercy is wider and deeper in Jewish thought than in ours. In the Old Testament it is the 'steadfast love' (*RSV*) which binds God to man and man to man.

yet mercy triumphs over judgment: or, boasts over judgment, i.e., as superior. The translation in the text brings out better the parallel with the original teaching of Jesus on the subject: cf. Lk. 6.37ff.; Mt. 7.1ff.: 'Not only is the execution of judgment held up: the judgment itself is withdrawn' (T. W. Manson).

14ff. *Faith and works:* cf. the Introduction above, pp. 16ff.

14. What does it profit: i.e., What good does it do?

if a man says he has faith. Faith is an inward bent of the real man, his fundamental attitude. It cannot exist without outward expression.

works: used in the Johannine literature for the outward acts which show the likeness of the Son to the Father and so reveal God. Here **works** are the outward expression of **faith**: the two go together like the obverse and reverse of a coin. James' doctrine is a favourite also with the author of 1 John: cf. 1 Jn 2.4, 'He who says "I know him" but disobeys his commandments is a liar, and the truth is not in him', cf. 6, 'He who says he abides in him ought to walk in the same way in which he walked', and 4.20; also 3.17.

Paul's 'faith working (i.e., being effective) through love' (Gal. 5.6) is the same idea.

15–19. Cf. 1 Jn 3.17, 'But if anyone has the world's goods and sees his brother in need, yet closes his heart against him, how does God's love abide in him?' Here 'faith' takes on the connotation it has in the Synoptics, the inner attitude which enables God to achieve outward results (cf. 'Your faith has made you well', Mk 5.34); this must involve real effort. The demons believe with an intensity of conviction that makes them shudder (verse 19), as before the Lord in his ministry (Mk 1.24, etc.); the difference between them and true believers is not that their faith is 'mere intellectual assent' but that it is of a quality that does not issue in works of love. It can only turn back on itself and make them 'shudder'.

15. daily food: food sufficient for even one day.

16. Go in peace: ordinary Jewish expression for 'goodbye'. For the notion of

things needed for the body, what does it profit? [17] So faith by itself, if it has no works, is dead.

18 But some one will say, 'You have faith and I have works.' Show me your faith apart from your works, and I by my works will show you my faith.[19] You believe that God is one; you do well. Even the demons believe—and shudder.[20] Do you want to be shown, you foolish fellow, that faith apart from works is barren? [21] Was not Abraham our father justified by works, when he offered his son

---

judgment according to works, cf. Mt. 25.34ff.; cf. Rom. 2.6 quoting Prov. 24.12; also Mt. 16.27; 1 C. 3.8; 2 C. 5.10.

17. by itself: or, possibly, 'in itself', i.e., faith is dead in itself if it does not issue in works. A different expression is used in verse 24 for 'by itself', 'only'.

18. Faith and works are not conceivable in separation, and cannot be the alternative prerogatives of different people: faith is that which leads to works and they prove its existence (cf. on 2.14f. above). Only here and at 2.14; 3.1 does the writer appear to speak in his own person—'I will show you my faith', 'my brethren'; but the device is purely rhetorical and gives no information about him. For the thought, cf. 2 Esd. 9.7.

19. that God is one: the fundamental affirmation of Jewish religion. It is no mere intellectual conviction, but a positive principle, involving that the whole of one's powers be devoted to God's service ('Thou shalt love the Lord thy God with all thy heart, with all thy soul, and with all thy strength'), that we must love all men alike because all are equal (God is not divided against himself and has no favourites) and that there can be no conflict between different sides of our nature or, fundamentally, between different duties (e.g., between faith and works).

the demons believe and shudder: it is the unity of God involving the exclusion of alien forces that makes them shudder: it is thus a burning reality that involves their destruction. The notion of demons shuddering is common: the Orphic fragment quoted in Clem. Alex. *Strom.* V.14 comes close to this verse in James, as does Justin Martyr, *Dial.* 49 (cf. on 2.15–19 above).

20. The argument from Scripture follows.

You foolish fellow: cf. Mt. 5.22; 1 C. 15.36. The imaginary interlocutor of the diatribe is addressed.

barren: idle, useless.

21. Abraham our Father: cf. 1 Clem. 31.2 which seems to be dependent on this passage: see the Introduction, p. 13. Abraham is a stock instance, used elsewhere (see on verse 23).

justified: introduced suddenly as a familiar term, in apparent reference to Paul's teaching (see on verse 24); but apart from this passage there is no reason to connect

Isaac upon the altar? [22] You see that faith was active along with his works, and faith was completed by works, [23] and the scripture was fulfilled which says, 'Abraham believed God, and it was reckoned to him as righteousness'; and he was called the friend of God. [24] You see that a man is justified by works and not by faith alone. [25] And in the same way was not also Rahab the harlot justified by works when she received the messengers and sent them out another way? [26] For

---

the two writers. The term was not original to Paul. It means the same in this verse as 'save' in verse 14.

22. The whole emphasis of verses 14ff., 18f. is repeated: faith and works are concurrent and complementary.

23. James does not necessarily imply that the story of the offering of Isaac (Gen. 22.1–14) and the passage quoted in this verse (Gen. 15.6) are related in the Old Testament; he means that the truth of the latter was demonstrated in the former. This is in keeping with rabbinic modes of exegesis, wherein distant passages are related. On the other hand James may mean that the earlier Genesis passage was a prophecy fulfilled in the second. The faith of Abraham in other New Testament books is shown in various ways: Rom. 4.17ff. confidence in the promise of a son; Heb. 11.8ff. in his departure to an unknown country; and again Heb. 11.17ff. in his readiness to sacrifice Isaac (cf. 1 Clem. 31).

the friend of God: apparently one of a series of similar titles for Abraham; cf. Isa. 41.8 (Heb.). On the possibility that 1 Clem. 10.1 may quote this passage, see the Introduction. It is unlikely that the last sentence of verse 23 is entirely otiose: friendship with God is reckoned as willing his will, as in the Johannine literature, and as 'being justified' is interpreted as faith manifested in works. Being 'justified' has the sense 'being proved right'.

24. by faith alone: the idea seems peculiar to Paul and this verse. The formula 'justified by faith' in fact only occurs once in the Pauline letters themselves outside Galatians and Romans, namely in Phil. 3.9, 'a righteousness . . . which is through faith in Christ'. For the significance of this, see the Introduction pp. 16ff.

Two aspects of Jesus' teaching are emphasized by Paul and James respectively: and these are represented by the parable of the Pharisee and the Publican (Lk. 18.10ff, note especially 14) and the passages Mt. 7.21ff., 24ff.; Lk. 6.46ff.; Mt. 21.28ff.; Mk 3.34f. (cf. Jn 7.17; Lk. 16.31; Jn 14.15, etc.).

25. Rahab is, like Abraham, a stock illustration: Jos. 2.1–21, etc.; Heb. 11.31; 1 Clem. 12. In Mt. 1.5 she is an ancestress of our Lord. Her faith, put into words in Jos. 2.11, is expressed in her relationship with the spies.

26. James is thinking here of the *unity* of faith and works; had he been thinking of works as an *expression* of faith, the analogy would have been better the other way round, faith = spirit, works = body. He simply means that just as, when the

as the body apart from the spirit is dead, so faith apart from works is
dead.

3 Let not many of you become teachers, my brethren, for you
know that we who teach shall be judged with greater strictness.
[2] For we all make many mistakes, and if any one makes no mistakes
in what he says he is a perfect man, able to bridle the whole body
also. [3] If we put bits into the mouths of horses that they may obey us,
we guide their whole bodies. [4] Look at the ships also; though they

---

spirit has departed from the body it is dead, so a man is inwardly dead if he has
no 'works' to show.
spirit: the vital principle, cf. Jn 19.30 with Mk 15.37.

FURTHER MORAL EXHORTATIONS 3.1–5.12

Chapter 3 shows considerable Hellenistic influence. Some have thought that a
separate document was incorporated at this point.

1. teachers: the position of teachers in the Christian Church was one of honour:
Rom. 12.7; Ac. 13.1; 1 Tim. 3.2; Tit. 1.9: *Didache* 11.1f. James warns against too
lightly taking on the responsibility. The next few verses leave the question of
teaching altogether, and treat of the dangers of talkativeness, as though this
verse had read, 'Do not talk too much'. Matthew's special source contained a
warning concerning the dangers that beset those who call themselves 'rabbis':
Mt. 23.8; and Paul warns the Jew who, 'instructed in the Law', is sure that he
is 'a guide to the blind, a light to those who are in darkness, a corrector of the
foolish, a teacher of children . . .' that he will be expected to practise what he
preaches.

we who teach: James himself is a teacher. His epistle is an example of the kind of
instruction given by such persons in the Church.

shall be judged with greater strictness: at the last judgment. Cf. Lk. 12.47f.,
appropriate to Jewish teachers but directed also at those having responsibility in
the Church; and Jn 9.41.

2. Cf. Mt. 12.35ff. and especially 36f.: the mouth speaks from the overflow of
the heart, so that in the judgment idle words will convict, i.e., by showing what
manner of man the speaker was (cf. also Sir. 5.13).

perfect: see 1.4 and note.

bridle: a favourite metaphor with Hellenistic moralists.

3. bits: the same word means bridles; hence the connection with the previous
verse. The part which goes in the horse's mouth is the most important for con-
trolling and guiding the whole animal.

are so great and are driven by strong winds, they are guided by a
very small rudder wherever the will of the pilot directs. ⁵ So the
tongue is a little member and boasts of great things. How great a
forest is set ablaze by a small fire!

6 And the tongue is a fire. The tongue is an unrighteous world
among our members, staining the whole body, setting on fire the
cycle of nature, and set on fire by hell. ⁷ For every kind of beast and

---

4. The metaphors of horse and ship are frequent in Greek writers, often in
combination. The rudder, though small like the tongue, is a most important part
of the ship. The man in control of it controls the whole vessel (cf. verse 2).
pilot: helmsman.

5. The tongue is as dangerous as a fire in a forest. Another familiar metaphor.

6. unrighteous world: lit., world (*kosmos*) of iniquity; cf. 1 Enoch 48.7 'this
world of iniquity'; Gal. 1.4, 'this present evil world (age)'; *Lev. Rab.* 26 (124c),
'When I was with you, I was in a world of falsehood . . . but I am in a world of
truth', i.e., the next world. For 'world' in James, see on 1.27 and 4.4. But this
makes very little sense unless the writer is thinking of the expression he used at 1.27,
'unstained from the world', when he would mean that the staining world is
represented in our natures by the tongue; it is here that its corrupting influence
makes itself felt, since the other members are dumb.

The Vulgate translates 'the whole world [*universitas*] of evil', which is perhaps
the most obvious way to read it (cf. Prov. 17.6 LXX, 'the faithful has the whole
world of wealth', for this use of *kosmos*, the only occurrence of this meaning) but
it cannot be said to fit the context any better.

The third possible interpretation is to make *kosmos* mean 'ornament', as it does
in 1 Pet. 3.3., and translate, 'the tongue puts a fair complexion on iniquity'. But
this also does not fit.

Many think the text corrupt and emend in various ways by substituting for
'world' some word meaning 'source' or the like, or by omitting 'the unrighteous
world' or 'the tongue a fire; the unrighteous world' as a title of the section which
has crept into the text (the remaining Greek stands by itself). This, however,
involves the necessity of leaving out also 'staining the whole body' as not appropriate to a fire, or the tongue. The Peshitta Syriac reads, 'the tongue is a fire; the
evil world is a forest'; but this is probably a conjecture also.

staining: cf. 1.27, 'unstained from the world'.

whole body: see verse 3 above. 'Body' for the Jew can mean 'person, personality'.
The tongue stains the whole person because it formulates desires and designs
which may be evil. Cf. Mk 7.20f.: 'He [Jesus] said, 'What comes out of a man is
what defiles a man. For from within, out of the heart [mind] of man, come evil
thoughts, fornication, theft, murder," etc.'.

bird, of reptile and sea creature, can be tamed and has been tamed by human-kind, **8** but no human being can tame the tongue—a restless evil full of deadly poison. **9** With it we bless the Lord and Father, and with it we curse men, who are made in the likeness of God. **10** From the same mouth come blessing and cursing. My brethren, this ought not to be so. **11** Does a spring pour forth from the same opening fresh water and brackish? **12** Can a fig tree, my brethren, yield olives, or a grapevine figs? No more can salt water yield fresh.

---

cycle of nature: originally an Orphic phrase connected with reincarnation: 'wheel of fate and birth' (Simplicius, sixth century A.D.), apparently watered down to mean 'the course of existence', 'the round of human life', as here. James would have nothing to do with 'fate', and the tongue could scarcely set on fire the endless cycle of rebirth. In Buddhism the phrase had a more pessimistic connotation than in Greek circles.

setting on fire . . . and set on fire by hell: Hell is *Gehenna*, transliterated only here in the Greek New Testament (*RSV* margin) outside Jesus' teaching as recorded in the Synoptic Gospels. The fire of hell is connected with the destructive fire of sin, as two sides of the same thing. Judgment works here without the direct intervention of God. See on 1.17ff. and 4.12.

7. tamed by humankind: or tamed in subjection to humankind, cf. Gen. 1.26 and verse 9 below, where James has the same context in mind.

8. Man can tame the animals, but not his own unruly nature as typified by the tongue.

restless: as opposed to tameable. Another reading is 'uncontrollable'.

9. the Lord and Father: a phrase for which there is no complete parallel. Both words apparently refer to God the Father.

we curse: James includes himself among sinful men who bless and curse but presumably practises what he preaches in verse 10.

in the likeness of God: James' ethics have a two-fold basis: man is to share God's character (1.18, 20; cf. Lk. 6.35) and respect the dignity of man as God made him (2.1ff.; 5.1ff.; cf. Mt. 25.35ff.). Jesus' teaching on not cursing men stresses the first factor in Lk. 6.28, 35, but in the other version of his sayings even this is connected explicitly with God's creatorhood and not with some special Gospel dispensation (Mt. 5.45).

10. Cf. *Test. Benj.* 6, 'The good mind has not two tongues, of blessing and cursing'; *Lev. Rab.* 33 (130b): 'from it [the tongue] comes good and bad, the best and the worst.'

11. fresh water and brackish: lit., sweet and bitter. Cf. 'a spring of light' and 'a fountain of darkness' in 1QS 3.19. The Latin proverb reads, *A fonte puro pura defluit aqua*; but see Lucretius: *De Rerum Natura* 4.1133 on sexual love: 'From the

13 Who is wise and understanding among you? By his good life let him show his works in the meekness of wisdom. ¹⁴ But if you have bitter jealousy and selfish ambition in your hearts, do not boast and be false to the truth. ¹⁵ This wisdom is not such as comes down from above, but is earthly, unspiritual, devilish. ¹⁶ For where

---

heart of the fountain of delight there rises a jet of bitterness that tortures us among the flowers themselves.' The question of this verse could be James' text for his doctrine of consistency in God and man.

12. The same idea as in Mt. 7.16; 12.33; but not dependent on those passages.

TRUE WISDOM 3.13-18

13. wise and understanding: practically synonymous. The word for 'wise' is the technical term for a teacher and recalls the Sage of the Wisdom literature. This is the connection with the preceding verses (cf. 3.1).

meekness of wisdom: see on 1.5, 21. Jewish writers stress the need for humility in teachers: *Aboth* 4.12, R. Meir said, 'Lessen your labour for worldly goods, and occupy yourself with Torah; be humble of spirit before all men'.

14. To claim wisdom without meekness is to be false to the truth— which is not a matter for boasting.

selfish ambition: one word in the Greek. It also signifies 'rivalry'.

the truth. In the light of the meaning of 'wisdom' (see on 1.5) 'truth' refers to 'true living' cf. 1 Jn 1.6, 'we lie, and do not [live according to] the truth'.

15. wisdom . . . such as comes down from above: cf. 1.5, 17, 'If any of you lacks wisdom, let him ask God who gives to all men generously and without reproaching . . . Every good endowment and every perfect gift is from above . . .', and verse 17 below. For the expression **'from above'** see especially the Fourth Gospel, which appears to use it where the Wisdom literature has 'from the highest': cf. Wis. 6.3 with Jn 19.11; Wis. 9.17 with Jn 3.7.

earthly: cf. Jn 3.31; 8.23. In John the contrast heaven (from above)—earth is used; cf. Wis. 9.16 and on 'from above' in the first part of this verse; also Matthew's favourite distinction 'heaven-earth', Mt. 5.34f.; 6.19f. *al.*

unspiritual: lit. 'psychic', 'belonging to the soul', but meaning, in the New Testament, physical (i.e., of life in men and animals). Man was divided into body soul, and spirit, the latter being the self. There is no reason to see in these verses the gnostic distinction between the lower grades of men as 'earthly' and 'physical'.

devilish: demonic. The 'wisdom' that men boast of and that causes dissension and rivalry is not from above but belongs to the earthly, physical world, peopled and largely controlled by demons.

In this passage James is opposing those who have pretensions to wisdom which produce bitter jealousy and rivalry. The reference is evidently to the 'many

jealousy and selfish ambition exist, there will be disorder and every vile practice. ¹⁷ But the wisdom from above is first pure, then peaceable, gentle, open to reason, full of mercy and good fruits, without uncertainty or insincerity. ¹⁸ And the harvest of righteousness is sown in peace by those who make peace.

---

teachers' of 5.1, though the present verse might countenance the view that some professed a superior wisdom 'from above' (cf. Rom. 1.22; 1 C. 1.19ff.).

16. vile: worthless, base, evil simply as the opposite of good, and without reference to any particular sort of badness.

17f. This passage closely resembles in style Wis. 7.22ff.

from above: see on verse 15 above.

pure: cf. Wis. 7.25. The word signifies what is undefiled or innocent in every sense. Wisdom is like light, penetrating everywhere yet not polluted by its contact with earthly objects. This purity is then split up by James into the different colours, peace, gentleness, etc.

peaceable: cf. Mt. 5.9; Gal. 5.22; Rom. 12.18; Eph. 6.15; Heb. 12.14, etc.

gentle: reasonable, sensible, kind, forbearing. A typically Greek virtue, but, like the others in the list, translating what is characteristic of Christianity (cf. e.g., Mt. 5.5; 10.16; Gal. 5.22).

open to reason: compliant, reasonable.

mercy: see on 2.13 and Mt. 5.7. Under rabbinic law there is a limit to charity, but none to the 'bestowal of lovingkindness'.

good fruits: cf. Mt. 7.16–20 and verse 12 above, which refers to the same teaching; also Gal. 5.22.

without uncertainty: translated in 1.6 'with no doubting' again in reference to Wisdom. Here it may mean 'impartial', cf. the situation in 2.1ff.; or 'whole-hearted', with reference to 3.9–12. But lists of virtues like this have no necessary reference to context.

insincerity: 'hypocrisy'.

18. the harvest of righteousness, etc.: lit., fruit, i.e. what righteousness produces: cf. Isa. 32.17 'the work of righteousness shall be peace'; and so in other Old Testament passages; or 'the righteous harvest', which creates a less cumbersome combination of ideas; and there is no hint that 'the product of righteousness' here is anything other than righteousness itself (cf. Heb. 12.11). 'Jealousy and selfish ambition' produce 'disorder and every vile practice' (cf. 16 above); but peacemakers sowing in peace reap a harvest that is righteousness (cf. Mt. 5.9; Col. 1.20). Jewish literature contains many references to the duty of peacemaking: cf. *Aboth* 1.22, 'Be of the disciples of Aaron, loving peace and pursuing peace, loving thy fellow-creatures'; *Peah* 1.1, 'making (lit. bringing) peace between a man and his fellow'.

4 What causes wars, and what causes fightings among you? Is it
not your passions that are at war in your members? ² You desire
and do not have; so you kill. And you covet and cannot obtain; so
you fight and wage war. You do not have, because you do not ask.
³ You ask and do not receive, because you ask wrongly, to spend it

---

by those: or, '*for those* who make peace'.

CALL TO REPENTANCE 4.1–10

1. The thought of peace contrasts with the prevailing conditions of war.
wars . . . fightings: the words are used of internal quarrels, and except perhaps
here, 'fightings' always refers to such in the New Testament; cf. 2 C. 7.5; 2 Tim.
2.23f.; Tit. 3.9; and 1 Clem. 46.5, 'Why are there strifes and wraths and dis-
sensions and schisms and war among you?' Nevertheless they remain meta-
phorical: the examples adduced are ambiguous. If the epistle is in the style of the
diatribe, aimed at no particular group, the words 'among you' have a general
reference. In this case the verse covers all kinds of fighting: cf. (with Mayor) the
literal meaning of 'you kill' in verse 2; and Plato, *Phaedo* 66C for the whole
section, 'Nothing else but the body and its desires produce wars and seditions and
battles'. Grotius would then be justified in applying this verse to international
affairs. But it could hardly be addressed to a congregation of the first Christians,
who boasted of having left such fighting behind: e.g., Justin, 1 *Apol.* 39.1ff.,
'We, who formerly killed one another, now not only do not make war upon our
enemies, but, so as not to lie or deceive those who examine us, gladly die, confessing Christ'. They held that this was in fulfilment of the 'swords into plough-
shares' prophecy of Isa. 2.3f.: cf. *Dial.* 728f. (Migne, *PG*); Irenaeus, *Adv.Haer.*
IV.34.4, who says that this was effected by the 'law of liberty, that is, the word of
God' (cf. Jas 1.25). See also Justin, 1 *Apol.* 14.3.
passions: lit., pleasures; but also lusts, desires, and this fits the context better.
at war: not within each person, but between persons.
members: equivalent to 'bodies', cf. Rom. 6.13, 'Do not yield your members to
sin as weapons of unrighteousness'; 7.5, 23; Col. 3.5.
2. kill: Erasmus made the conjectural emendation *phthoneite* (envy) for *pho-
neuete* (kill). Support is given to this if **you covet** is translated 'you are jealous'.
But cf. 1 Pet. 4.15.
You do not have because you do not ask: cf. Mt. 7.7ff. The conviction of the
goodness of God traces the cause of want to lack of single-minded desire (1.7f.).
3. You ask: the word is in a different voice from that in the previous verse and
that following, and may imply a request considered as a mere form, without the
spirit of prayer (so Mayor).

on your passions. ⁴ Unfaithful creatures! Do you not know that friendship with the world is enmity with God? Therefore whoever wishes to be a friend of the world makes himself an enemy of God. ⁵ Or do you suppose it is in vain that the scripture says, 'He yearns jealously over the spirit which he has made to dwell in us'? ⁶ But he gives more grace; therefore it says, 'God opposes the proud, but

---

wrongly, to spend it on your passions: a further reason is now given for want, namely that prayer is made for the wrong reasons. This follows the line of the Jewish (and Platonic) teaching that God only hears the righteous (cf. Ps. 34.15; 145.18; Prov. 10.24; 15.29; Jn 9.31; 11.42; 16.23f.; 1 Jn 5.14, etc.).

4. Unfaithful creatures: lit., 'adulteresses'. Adultery was a term equivalent to idolatry, God being thought of as the husband of his people. Fornication is used in the same way (cf. Ps. 106.39; Jer. 3.6ff., 20; Ezek, 16 *passim*; Hos. 2 *passim*; Rev. 14.8; etc.). Jesus speaks of an 'adulterous [unfaithful] and sinful generation' (Mk 8.38; cf. Mt. 12.39). Sometimes the individuals comprising the people of God are spoken of in this way: Exod. 34.15; Num. 15.39; Ps. 73.27; Hos. 4.12. But the whole nation is in mind each time; the individual spoken of alone (as in this verse in James, and in the feminine, to indicate the individual soul as the bride of God) is unusual.

friendship with the world: for 'world' see on 1.27; 2.5; 3.6; cf. also Jn 12.25, where a familiar saying of Jesus receives a new twist; 15.19; 1 Jn 2.15; 3.13; Mt. 10.22, etc. The notion follows naturally upon that of unfaithfulness to God amid surrounding idolatry, exaltation of false ideals; but it is the Church against the world, not Judaism against Greek culture.

enmity with God . . .an enemy of God: the enmity is not on God's side but on that of the man who makes himself 'a friend of the world'.

5. Or introduces an argument supplementary to the previous argument.

the scripture: no such passage occurs in the Bible or the Apocrypha. Various explanations have been attempted, some involving the excision of 'He yearns . . . more grace' as a parenthesis, so that the scriptural quotation begins at 'God opposes the proud' in verse 6, others making the sentence a free citation or rough summary of various Old Testament passages (Gen. 6.3; Exod. 20.3, 5; Isa. 63.8–15; Zech. 1.14; 8.2 or the quotation from Proverbs in verse 6), others again proposing conjectural emendations of the text. Three or four renderings are also possible of the verse, for which see *RV* text and margin. The most obvious one as opposed to the *RSV* is 'The spirit which he has made to dwell in us yearns jealously'. For the view that the 'scripture' referred to is the Dead Sea 'Manual of Discipline' (1QS), see below on **spirit**. Spitta held that the quotation is from the Book of Eldad and Modad (cf. Num. 11.29, where the issue is envy), cited in Hermas, *Vis.* 2.3.4, and (as 'scripture') probably in 1 Clem. 23.2f. and 2 Clem. 11.2ff. Jas 4.8 is identical in substance with the quotation in Hermas ('The Lord is near those who turn to him') and the *Num. Rab.* 15 mentions the greater grace given to Eldad and Modad because of their humility: cf. verse 6 and on 1.7f. See also Hermas *Mand.* 3.1 'the spirit which God caused to dwell in this flesh' for the form of this verse (cf. Introduction, p. 12).

jealously: or enviously. The word is not used in the LXX for the 'jealousy' of God; and it usually refers to hatred of the person who has the coveted object.

spirit: this could refer simply to the spirit in man (cf. Mk 14.38 and Gen. 2.7), or to the Holy Spirit. In the DSS men are graded 'according to their spirits': 1QS 2.20; 3.14; 4.6–26; 5.21–24; 6.17; 7.18–23; 9.14, 15, 18. The 'two spirits' in man, one bad and one good, also figure (1QS 3.25ff.) and also the term 'holy spirit' (as in *Test. Jud.* 20), though 'the spirit of God' (or 'from God') or 'the spirit of the world' never occurs. *The Testaments of the Twelve Patriarchs* are nearer to New Testament language about the Holy Spirit: *Test. Naph.* 10.9, 'Blessed is the man who does not defile the holy Spirit of God which has been put and breathed into him': cf. and contrast Eph. 4.30. The ambiguity as to whether God's or man's spirit is intended in James is perpetuated in Hermas, *Mand.* 3.1: 'Love truth . . . that the spirit that God has made to dwell in this flesh may be found true by all men, and so the Lord who dwells in you will be glorified . . .' For the contrast in Paul, cf. 1 C. 2.11f., and Rom. 8.9f., where the indwelling Spirit involves the indwelling of Christ. Here in James the Spirit of God could be intended, if the quotation in the second half of the verse be taken as a question, 'Does the spirit which he made to dwell in us lust enviously?'

The pejorative sense usual with 'jealously' plus the previous references to human desire (4.2, etc. and 'passions', i.e., desires, in 4.1, etc.) and the contrast apparently intended with the following words 'but he gives more grace' suggest that the human spirit is meant, and the rendering, 'The spirit which he [God] made to dwell in us lusts enviously' (cf. *NEB*). Gaster compares 1QS 4.9ff., where the spirit of perversion presented to man by God is associated with 'proud jealousy' among other things; but the context is no closer to James than any of those variously suggested from the Old Testament and in James the spirit could not have been created evil by God (1.17ff.). The alteration of one letter in the Greek for 'caused to dwell in us' would make it 'dwells in us', as some MSS, in fact, read.

6. he gives more grace: i.e. greater grace. This may be part of the quotation from 'scripture': 'The spirit which he made to dwell in us lusts enviously, but he gives greater grace.' The Proverbs quotation in the second half of the verse uses the word 'grace' in the sense of 'favour', which it commonly has; but it can scarcely mean this here in James. More probably it signifies 'help' (cf. Heb. 4.16). So in later thought, 'grace' comes to mean 'imparted inner power' as well as 'unmerited goodwill'.

the scripture says: lit., 'it says', a customary way of introducing a quotation.

'God opposes', etc.: quoted from Prov. 3.34 LXX, with 'God' substituted for 'the Lord' as in 1 Pet. 5.5 and 1 Clem. 30.2. The sentiment was common: cf.

gives grace to the humble.' ⁷ Submit yourselves therefore to God· Resist the devil and he will flee from you. ⁸ Draw near to God and he will draw near to you. Cleanse your hands, you sinners, and purify your hearts, you men of double mind. ⁹ Be wretched and mourn and weep. Let your laughter be turned to mourning and your joy to dejection. ¹⁰ Humble yourselves before the Lord and he will exalt you.

Lk. 14.11; 18.14; Mt. 23.12; Mk 18.4; Aristeas 257 ('It is a recognized principle that God by his very nature accepts the humble and the human race loves those who are willing to be in subjection to them' [Andrews in Charles].); 263; *Erub.* 13b. ('Who lowers himself, God will exalt'); Ezek. 21.31; 1 Sam. 2.7f.; Lk. 1.51f., etc **the proud:** the arrogant, who ride roughshod over others, and despise the righteous poor (cf. 1.10; 2.5ff.; 5.1ff. and Ps. 31.23).

the humble: before God and man; also lowly members of the community: 1.10; 2.5. (Cf. Mt. 5.3, 5.)

7. Submit yourselves therefore to God: i.e., obey God (cf. 1 Pet. 5.6).

Resist the devil: cf. 1 Pet. 5.9, preceded, as in James, with the quotation from Prov. 3.34; Hermas, *Mand.* 12.5.2, 'If you resist him [the devil] he will flee from you defeated and shamed'; *Test. Naph.* 8.4, 'If you do what is good . . . the devil will flee from you'; *Test. Iss.* 7.7, etc.

8. Draw near, etc.: cf. Zech. 1.3, 'Return to me, says the Lord of hosts, and I will return to you', and the similar sentiment in Mal. 3.7; Ps. 145.18. Nearer is Hermas, *Vis.* 2.3.4, ' "The Lord is near those who turn to him", as it is written in Eldad and Modad, who prophesied to the people in the wilderness' (cf. on 1.8; 4.5, 14; 5.7).

Cleanse your hands . . . your hearts: cf. Ps. 24.4. The first expression does not refer to outward cleanliness, as the parallelism with 'Purify your hearts' shows; both mean 'Be blameless, innocent' (cf. Job 22.30), especially of blood: Ps. 26.6, 9f.,' I wash my hands in innocence . . . Sweep me not away with sinners, nor my life with bloodthirsty men, men in whose hands are evil devices, and whose right hands are full of bribes'. See also Mt. 5.8 and Jas 5.1ff. for the sins the writer has in mind.

9. Be wretched and mourn: cf. 5.1ff. for the reasons behind James' vehemence, and also Lk. 6.24ff., 'Woe to you that are rich . . . to you that laugh now, for you shall mourn and weep'. The early Christians looked on the accepted things of this world with new eyes (cf. Lk. 16.15).

10. Humble yourselves, etc.: Lk. 14.11, 'He who humbles himself will be exalted' (the passive probably indicates that God is responsible, as here).

Carrington and Selwyn hold that much of the language in the above verses is taken from traditional catechisms, in which notions like submission could be

11 Do not speak evil against one another, brethren. He that speaks evil against a brother or judges his brother, speaks evil against the law and judges the law. But if you judge the law, you are not a doer of the law but a judge. 12 There is one lawgiver and judge, he who is able to save and destroy. But who are you that you judge your neighbour?

13 Come now, you who say, 'Today or tomorrow we will go into such and such a town and spend a year there and trade and get gain'; 14 whereas you do not know about tomorrow. What is your

---

applied in differing circumstances, to God (as here) or to man (1 Pet. 2.13) or to a husband (of the wife: Col. 3.18).

EVIL-SPEAKING 4.11–13

11. Do not speak evil: a common injunction (cf. Ps. 101.5; Wis. 1.11; 2 C· 12.20; Eph. 4.31; 1 Pet. 2.1, etc.). The parallelism indicates that criticism is meant' 'judging' (cf. Mt. 7.1).

speaks evil against the law: cf. *Dt. Rab.* 6 (203d): 'The man who slanders ultimately denies God' (cf. Jas 4.12).

judges the law: presumably the law that is summed up in the saying, 'You must love your neighbour as yourself', which assumes our equality before God and the law. So in the rest of the verse the slanderer and judger has ceased to obey the law and has become its critic.

12. God alone is the administrator of the law: in him only is vested the right of ultimate judgment. Who are *you* to judge? (cf. the end of the verse).

able to save and to destroy: cf. Mt. 10.28. Conventional words which ill-accord with the doctrine of 1.17ff. but the point stressed is that God is the ultimate power as well as the ultimate court of appeal, not that he is destructive. The verse expressed the sense of the numinous in the face of final reality. The phrase occurs in Hermas (*Mand.* 12.6.3; *Sim.* 9.23.4); cf. Dt. 32.39; 1 Sam. 2.6; 2 Kg. 5.7; Ps. 68.20.

HUMILITY BEFORE GOD'S PROVIDENCE 4.13–16

Cf. Prov. 27.1, 'Do not boast about tomorrow, for you do not know what a day may bring forth'. The idea is the opposite of that in Mt. 6.34, which counsels not caution but unconcern for the morrow because it is unknown. Even so, the saying is out of line with the rest of Jesus' teaching on freedom from care on the ground of God's beneficence, and occurs in the special material of Matthew which has affinities with James. See also for the same idea Lk. 12.16–20; also 1 Enoch 97.8ff.

14. What is your life? i.e., What sort of existence is it?

life? For you are a mist that appears for a little time and then vanishes.
¹⁵ Instead you ought to say, 'If the Lord wills, we shall live and we
shall do this or that.' ¹⁶ As it is, you boast in your arrogance. All
such boasting is evil. ¹⁷ Whoever knows what is right to do and
fails to do it, for him it is sin.

5 Come now, you rich, weep and howl for the miseries that are
coming upon you. ² Your riches have rotted and your garments
are moth-eaten. ³ Your gold and silver have rusted, and their rust

---

a mist: smoke or steam. Cf. 1 Clem. 17.6, Abraham says, 'I am like vapour from
a pot'. The thought is similar to that in 1.9ff. and therefore typical of James.

15. If the Lord wills. The expression was common among the ancient Greeks
and is commanded in the Koran for common use among Arabs. It is not Jewish
either in the Bible or Talmud; the only examples given by Billerbeck are from
the very late *Alphabet of ben Sirach* (after the 11th century). Instances in the New
Testament are confined to the writings of Luke, Paul, and the author of Hebrews:
Ac. 18.21; 1 C. 4.19; 16.7; Rom. 1.10; Phil. 2.19, 24; Heb. 6.3.

16. arrogance: presumption of the creature in disregarding the Creator.

17. for him it is sin: i.e., it is a sin on his part; no scruples such as those dealt
with in Rom. 14 are implied. Cf. the reiterated 'it is sin for you' in Deuteronomy,
e.g., 15.9. For the general idea of doing what one knows to be right, see Jn 9.41.

DENUNCIATION OF THE RICH 5.1-6

Cf. 1.10f.; 2.2ff. This section is in prophetic style. It also contains echoes of the
teaching of Jesus. This is one of the very few places in the New Testament where
any reference is made to the iniquity of existing social conditions, but it shows that
Christians were not oblivious to them, particularly when natives of Palestine and
not representatives abroad of a foreign cult. For James the Christian faith is to be
worked out in love for others, especially the underprivileged (cf. 2.14ff. and
Gal. 5.6).

1. Cf. Isa. 13.6; 15.2f.; and, for the rest of the section, Am. 8.4-6; also Lk. 6.24ff.

**2f. Your riches . . . moth-eaten. Your gold and silver have rusted . . .
You have laid up treasure:** cf. Mt. 6.19f., 'Do not lay up for yourselves treasures
on earth, where moth and rust consume . . . lay up for yourselves treasures in
heaven . . .' Silver and gold do not rust; James is thinking only of the perishable
nature of riches. The rot has already set in; in the light of reality riches and display
are signs of decay rather than present glories and will be destroyed at the last
judgment, which by its nature is the removal of corruption.

their rust: the word also means poison; so the author's mind passes over to the

will be evidence against you and will eat your flesh like fire. You have laid up treasure for the last days. ⁴ Behold, the wages of the labourers who mowed your fields, which you kept back by fraud, cry out; and the cries of the harvesters have reached the ears of the Lord of hosts. ⁵ You have lived on the earth in luxury and in pleasure; you have fattened your hearts in a day of slaughter. ⁶ You

---

idea of the burning up of the flesh, from the outward canker to the canker of the soul.

evidence: cf. Job 16.8, where Job's gauntness is an outward and visible sign of his guilt.

against you: or, for you, i.e., the sign to you of your inner corruption, showing the reality of the matter.

like fire: this phrase may be attached to the next sentence.

You have laid up treasure: lit., 'you stored up', with no object. The Peshitta Syriac connects the preceding phrase, omitting the 'like'; with this emendation the whole would read, 'their rust (poison) will testify against you and eat into your very flesh, for you have stored up fire for the last days' (so Goodspeed). Cf. Rom. 2.5, 'You are storing up wrath for yourself on the day of wrath'.

for the last days: lit., in the last days, i.e., the days preceding the end, cf. verses 7f., but also verse 5. A different interpretation is possible if the sentence 'You have laid up treasure for the last days' is taken by itself, namely that in the parable of the Rich Fool (Lk. 12.20, 'This night your soul is required of you; and the things you have prepared, whose will they be?') and in the Jewish story of the man who ordered footwear for seven years when he only had seven days to live; cf. also Sir. 14.15ff.

4. Cf. Hermas, *Vis.* 3.9.6, which has many affinities with this passage.

Lord of Hosts: only here in the New Testament except in the quotation from Isa. 1.9 in Rom. 9.29 (cf. Isa. 5.9 LXX).

5. in luxury and in pleasure: the original is more forceful, 'self-indulgence and voluptuousness'.

hearts: here apparently for appetites. The heart for the Jew was the seat of the inner life, of the soul or mind.

in a day of slaughter: (or, 'the day of slaughter', i.e., the judgment that is coming upon such people). If the same translation of the Greek word *en* is used as at verse 3 (*for* the last days), which consistency would seem to demand, the result is, 'for the day of slaughter'; cf. 1 Enoch 94.9, 'You have become ready for the day of slaughter', i.e., like a stalled ox. But see on verse 3 above; the only tolerable translation in both places leaves out the reference to the actual day of judgment: the slaughter is that of the economic battlefield, which is itself a sign of the final woes but in which it is the labourers who suffer.

have condemned, you have killed the righteous man; he does not resist you.

7 Be patient, therefore, brethren, until the coming of the Lord. Behold, the farmer waits for the precious fruit of the earth, being patient over it until it receives the early and late rain. [8] You also be

---

6. You have killed the righteous man, etc.: cf. the remarks about the suffering righteous one in Wisdom 2 and 5, who is directly related to the unresisting suffering servant of 2 Isaiah (42.1ff.; 53.1ff., 7f., etc.). The righteous man is the type of all righteous behaviour, and is identified with the poor, as in the Psalms, Isaiah, and Jeremiah. Men like Stephen and James the Apostle, martyred by the Jews, may therefore be in mind; and there may be an oblique reference to the execution of Jesus; cf. Ac. 2.23; 3.14f., 'You denied the holy and righteous One . . . and killed . . .', and Jesus' non-resistance at his trial.

he does not resist you: cf. Mt. 5.39 and above. The idea (the words are different in Matthew and James) is of not setting oneself against another in hostility, cf. Hos. 1.6, where the word used in James for 'resist' is contrasted with 'to show mercy' (i.e., in the Hebrew sense of 'to love'), and Prov. 3.34, where it is contrasted with 'to show grace, favour'. The righteous one who is killed shows grace and love to his tormentor: cf. the quotation from Justin Martyr above at 4.1.

Exhortation to Patience and Moral Stability Before the Lord's Coming 7–12

7. Be patient, i.e., exercise forbearance and fortitude.

the coming of the Lord: apparently the Second Coming of Jesus. The same word *parousia* is used as is peculiar in the Gospels to Matthew's special source, but it is common throughout the New Testament (cf. Mt. 24.3, 27, 37, 39 and 1 Th. 3.13; 4.15; 5.23; 2 Th. 2.1, etc.). The word is used of the state visit of a king. *Test. Jud.* 22.2 has 'until the appearing [*parousia*] of the God of righteousness', which is omitted by the Armenian version and may be a Christian interpolation. The fact that the word seems to be Christian probably here excludes the notion that the coming of the Lord of hosts (verse 4) is intended as in the Old Testament (Mal. 3.2 and cf. Joel 2.1, 31; Mal. 4.5; Isa. 13.6, 9, etc.) but see on 2 Pet. 5.12 and cf. on 2 Pet. 1.16.

farmer . . . fruit: the metaphor for the advent of the Lord is typical of the Synoptic Gospels; cf. the parables of growth in Mt. 13; Mk 13.28f., which cf. with Jas 5.9; 1 Clem. 23.3ff.; 2 Clem. 11.2ff. (Eldad and Modad?).

the early and the late rain: cf. Dt. 11.14; Jer. 5.24, etc. The early rain begins in Palestine in autumn, the latter rain in spring, and both are matters of great concern to the farmer. Hence the patience involved. Uncertainty about these rains seems

patient. Establish your hearts, for the coming of the Lord is at hand.
⁹ Do not grumble, brethren, against one another, that you may not
be judged; behold, the Judge is standing at the doors. ¹⁰As an example
of suffering and patience, brethren, take the prophets who spoke in
the name of the Lord. ¹¹ Behold, we call those happy who were
steadfast. You have heard of the steadfastness of Job, and you have
seen the purpose of the Lord, how the Lord is compassionate and
merciful.

---

to be confined to the Palestine areas. The author writes as though from first-hand
experience of these conditions.

8. Establish your hearts: Be strong and have confidence.

the coming of the Lord is at hand: Nowhere else in the New Testament is the
word *parousia* used with a verb of motion. Cf. Mk 1.15, etc. for the same verb
translated 'at hand' used of the kingdom of God.

9. grumble: lit., groan. Not obviously connected with the context, though it is
possible to make the sense, 'Do not blame each other for the troubles of this
swiftly-passing time'.

that you may not be judged: or, lest you be judged; the same wording as at
Mt. 7.1; cf. Lk. 6.37, 'and you will not be judged'. The connection is weaker in
Matthew between the judging and the being judged. Cf. Jas 4.11, 'he that speaks
evil against a brother or judges his brother'. The thought is plainly the same in
James as in Matthew and is brought to mind by the image of the Judge at the doors.

the Judge is standing at the doors: cf. Mk 13.29 (or should the translation here
be 'it' referring to the kingdom of God understood? The chapter is composite);
Rev. 3.20 (but here Christ does not come as Judge).

10. example: elsewhere in the New Testament Jesus is the natural example:
Jn 13.15; 1 C. 11.1; 1 Th. 1.6; Heb. 12.2; 1 Pet. 2.21; cf. Mk 1:18, etc. But Heb. 11
also makes use of many other examples, as does 1 Clem. outside the canon.

prophets: cf. the following references to that killing of prophets in the New
Testament: Mt. 21.35f.; 22.6; 23.29–37; Lk. 13.33; Ac. 7.51f.; Rom. 11.3; 1 Th.
2.15; Heb. 11.35ff.; Rev. 11.7; 16.6; 18.24.

the Lord: i.e., the LORD of the Old Testament.

11. steadfast, steadfastness: the notion is rather that of those who went
through sufferings: Job was not in the least Stoical or unwavering. But he did
refuse to 'curse God and die' (Job 2.9) or blame God (Job 1.22; cf. Jas 1.12f.,
'Blessed is the man who endures trial . . . Let no one say when he is tempted, "I
am tempted by God"; for God cannot be tempted with evil and he himself tempts
no one'; also the rest of this verse).

purpose: lit., 'end', i.e., the happy ending of Job's troubles: Job 42.12, 'the Lord

12 But above all, my brethren, do not swear, either by heaven or by earth or with any other oath, but let your yes be yes and your no be no, that you may not fall under condemnation.

13 Is any one among you suffering? Let him pray. Is any cheerful? Let him sing praise. ¹⁴ Is any among you sick? Let him call for the elders of the church, and let them pray over him, anointing him with oil in the name of the Lord; ¹⁵ and the prayer of faith will save

---

blessed Job's last days'. For one who is confident of the goodness of God the end of the Book of Job is by no means an anti-climax but essential to the whole plot, even if expressed in terms naive to our taste: the Christian himself expects heaven, which is the happy ending to end all happy endings. Tragedy is ultimately non-Christian. Cf. *Test. Benj.* 4.1, 'You see, therefore, my children, the end of the good man'.

how the Lord is compassionate and merciful: the very purpose of trial, according to James, is that faith in God's goodness should become stronger and conquer the troubles themselves (1.4) even up to the final Coming itself.

compassionate: *very* kind. The word occurs elsewhere in early extant works only in Hermas, *Sim.* 5.7.4. It is related to the word for 'viscera', considered the seat of the feelings—of anger, anxiety, etc. in the Greek poets and of kindness and pity in the LXX, New Testament, and papyri.

merciful: the word used for the goodness of God which is held up for imitation in Lk. 6.36.

12. Do not swear, etc.: no more organically connected with the context than the injunction against complaining in verse 9 (cf. Mt. 5.33–37).

by heaven or by earth: *Sheb.* 4.13 actually states that such an oath was not binding upon a witness. Elliott-Binns thinks the omission of 'Jerusalem' (Mt. 5.35) may be evidence of a desire to minimize the prestige of that city. Kilpatrick holds that the saying as it stands in Matthew may be an expansion.

Let your yes be yes and your no be no: Mt. 5.37 is so quoted by Justin, Clement of Alexandria and others. Ropes holds that this form has been accommodated to a current Jewish phrase, on the basis of *Ruth Rab.* 3.18, 'With the righteous is their "yes" yes, and their "no" no' (cf. also *Mekilta* on Exod. 19.24). But the 'yes, yes', 'no, no' form of the saying was also current outside Christian circles: cf. the following from *The Book of the Secrets of Enoch* (2 Enoch): 'I swear not by any oath, neither by heaven nor by earth, nor by any other creature which God created. The Lord said, There is no oath in me, nor injustice, but truth. If there is no truth in men, let them swear by the words "yea, yea", or else "nay, nay".' Cf. Philo, *De Spec. Leg.* 2.1; *Leg. All.* 3.72, etc.; and for the repetition Num. 5.22; Neh. 8.16; Lk. 6.46; 10.41; 22.31. Thus both forms of the saying were current, and there is no means of deciding between them on this basis. One version seems to mean 'You do not need to say more than yes or no to establish the truth of a proposition', the other, 'Make your "yes" mean "yes" and your "no" mean "no"'. The former implies that anything extra is an attempt to dress up the truth, the latter that it is vacillation or insincerity.

that you may not fall under condemnation is parallel to 'whatever is more than this comes of evil' in Mt. 5.37.

PRAYER AND FAITH 5.13–18

13. suffering: in trouble.
cheerful: in good spirits.
Let him sing praise: cf. Eph. 5.19, lit., 'sing a psalm (or hymn)'.
pray: i.e., for relief.

14. elders: a typically Jewish title, though the word was used among Gentiles of civic and religious officials. Both synagogue and early Church were governed by elders (cf. 1 Pet. 5.1–5; Ac. 5.6, 10). In the former rules were laid down by the rabbis for the visitation of the sick, including exhortation to set his affairs in order and to make his confession if he were near to death. In the later Church the possession of a valid gift of healing was considered a qualification for ordination; bishops and elders were by virtue of their office possessed of this gift (Canons of Hippolytus, 17, 39, 53).

church: there is no evidence that the word was applied to the individual synagogue, though it could have been. In Christian Aramaic of a later date the same word did duty for both. In Ac. 5.11 the term 'church' is applied to the Christians in Jerusalem as a body. In Pauline usage it refers to individual communities in different places (1 Th. 1.1; 1 C. 1.2; Col. 4.16; cf. also Ac. 8.1). The same evidently applies here. See on 2.2.

oil: oil was used as a healing agent by various peoples including the Hebrews and was a symbol of joy (Ps. 45.7). The apostles of Jesus anointed with oil and healed sick people (Mk 6.13). The text in James is evidence that the practice was continued in the early Church, as we know it was later from references in the Fathers until, in medieval times, it was changed into the rite of extreme unction for those on the point of death.

in the name of the Lord: the demons were subject to the disciples in Jesus' name (Lk. 10.17). That moral and spiritual significance attached to this in the Lord's mind is shown by his answer to those who would forbid the strange exorcist (Mk 9.38f.). 'In his Name' brought the ailing person within the whole context of his continued ministry in the Church and into the world seen new as the sphere of his activity and as stemming from and dependent upon a God of like character. **The Lord** evidently means Jesus in this connection. As this verse shows, it is misleading to speak of oil having a purely medicinal use in the Church until the sacrament of extreme unction came into vogue: no such rationalistic separation is visible here. James' approach is theological.

the sick man, and the Lord will raise him up; and if he has committed sins, he will be forgiven. ¹⁶ Therefore confess your sins to one another, and pray for one another, that you may be healed. The prayer of a righteous man has great power in its effects. ¹⁷ Eli'jah

---

15. This verse reads like a rubric from a Church order.

the prayer of faith sounds like a technical term; it apparently corresponds to prayer and anointing 'in the name of the Lord' (cf. 1.2–6; 2.14ff.). As in the Synoptics, it is the **faith** that heals.

save: restore to health. The word has not necessarily the religious overtones it has for us. It can refer to rescue from natural danger or from disease.

the sick man . . . the Lord will raise him up: there is no suggestion that the man is dying or any question of raising him from death. He will be raised from his bed of sickness. **The Lord** may refer to Christ or the Father.

if he has committed sins: Jesus connected sin and sickness (Mk 2.5), though not as the Jews did (Jn 9.3). This must not be interpreted as a foreshadowing of modern psychological theory: the forgiveness is part of the total restoration of the person effected in healing. Nevertheless the confession has this therapeutic value.

he will be forgiven: lit., 'it will be forgiven him', suggestive of a formula of absolution (cf. Mk 2.5).

16. confess your sins to one another: the custom of confession before the whole congregation was operative in the early centuries (cf. *Didache* 4.14; 14.1; Tertullian, *De Poenit.* 9). But James has in mind confession of sins to the elders in the sick room; therefore the elders here are acting as part of the Church, in which resides the power to pronounce God's forgiveness.

that you may be healed: i.e., either 'so that you may be healed' or simply 'pray . . . to be healed'. The subordinate clause may be connected with both of the two main clauses or with the latter only. It is thus not clear whether or not the confession and intercessory prayer are to have equal shares in the result. The whole section gives a picture of a community in which the needs of the body and soul are taken as one problem and dealt with in the common life of the fellowship.

The prayer of a righteous man: part of the approach familiar in James' school: see on 4.3. The word translated 'prayer' has the more restricted meaning of 'petition'.

in its effects: four translations are possible: (*a*) 'when it begins to work' (as here); (*b*) 'when he tries' (cf. verse 17); (*c*) as an adjective attached to 'prayer', effective (so *AV* and *NEB*); (*d*) 'when it is made effective'. (*a*) and (*c*) add little to the sense; (*d*) could conceivably mean, 'given the opportunity', e.g., when the sick man calls upon the Church for prayer.

17. Elijah is taken as an example of the powers of a praying human being.

was a man of like nature with ourselves and he prayed fervently
that it might not rain, and for three years and six months it did not
rain on the earth. ¹⁸ Then he prayed again and the heaven gave rain,
and the earth brought forth its fruit.

19 My brethren, if any one among you wanders from the truth
and some one brings him back, ²⁰ let him know that whoever
brings back a sinner from the error of his way will save his soul from
death and will cover a multitude of sins.

---

of like nature: in the same position, with the same feelings and experiences
(cf. Ac. 14.15). Elijah is taken as a human example. The Epistle to the Hebrews
uses Jesus as an example of effective prayer (Heb. 5.7), and stresses the necessity to
us of his humanity (Heb. 2.14-17; 5.1-8).

prayed fervently: lit. 'prayed in prayer', which looks like an attempt to recall
the Hebrew infinitive absolute construction (cf. Lk. 22.14, 'with desire I have
desired' with Gen. 31.30 LXX). In 1 Kg. 17.1 Elijah prophesies that it will not
rain, but does not pray (nor does he pray for the drought to cease; but cf. 1 Kg.
18.42), though prayer is stressed in his other miracles (1 Kg. 17.21; 18.37).

three years and six months: cf. Lk. 4.25. The exact period is not mentioned in
the Old Testament, but is a reasonable deduction from 1 Kg. 18.1, 'After many
days, the word of the Lord came to Elijah *in the third year*'. The only existent
Midrash on the latter passage counts only three months out of the first and third
years, thus bringing the time down to eighteen months, and is followed in this by
the *Yalkut Shimeoni*, 1:210. Dalman points out that Windisch (and, we might add,
Ropes) wrongly takes this to mean three and a half years. He, in his turn, amasses a
collection of passages to show that 'three and a half years' was a conventional
term for 'a considerable period' (so also G. Kittel, as Dalman notes). In Daniel on
the other hand (7.25; 12.7) the idea is probably 'half of seven' (the 'perfect'
number).

19. the truth: cf. Dan. 9.13; Sir. 4.28; Jn *passim*, e.g., 8.32; 18.37, etc.; 2 Th.
2.10; Gal. 5.7, etc. It is quite misleading to quote Greek philosophical texts over
against the factual Hebrew notion of truth; the ordinary meaning in the two
languages coincides: truth=what is true as opposed to false, insincere, superficial.
(See further ,J. Barr, *Semantics of Biblical Language*, pp. 187ff.) A comparison with
'the error of his way' suggests the notion of 'true way': cf. Jn 14.6, 'I am the way,
and the truth, and the life', where Moffatt translates, 'true and living way' (See
Heb. 10.20).

brings him back: lit., 'turns him'. This meaning is rare in Greek and corresponds
to the Hebrew meaning to turn back and to repent.

20. his soul: i.e., the soul of the erring brother. Cf. 1.21.

death: the word indicates the seriousness of departing from the Christian way. Inside were healing and forgiveness, outside death and guilt. Cf. 1.15.

will cover a multitude of sins: 'cover' or 'hide' used of sin means to obliterate or cause to be forgotten (i.e. by God) in the Old Testament: see Ps. 32.1f.; 85.2. But that is not the meaning in Prov. 10.12 (cf. 1 Pet. 4.8; 1 Clem. 49.5), from which this quotation is taken. There it means that love does not stir up matter for recrimination: cf. Prov. 17.9, 'He who covers an offence seeks love'. The expression has apparently become quite conventional, and seems to mean here simply 'will undo a great deal of harm'.

The relation between the two writings called the Epistle of Jude and
the second Epistle of Peter is close. The latter reproduces the thought
and much of the phraseology (though only in one brief phrase
exactly) of the former, especially in chapter 2. The same sequence of
examples from the Old Testament is kept (with the addition of
Noah): the fallen angels, the cities of Sodom and Gomorrah, Balaam.
For these, compare 2 Pet. 2.4 with Jude 1.6 (angels); 2 Pet. 2.6–9
with Jude 7 (Sodom and Gomorrah); 2 Pet. 2.10f. with Jude 8ff.
(return to the angel theme); 2 Pet. 2.15f. with Jude 11 (Balaam).
Only 2 Peter and Jude in the New Testament use such lists of Old
Testament characters as prototypes of their opponents. Other
resemblances also occur in the same order: the false teachers who
deny the Lord (2 Pet. 2.1=Jude 4; the same word *despotēs*, master,
being used of Jesus as is rarely used elsewhere); the troublemakers'
defilement and disparagement of authority (2 Pet. 2.10f.=Jude 8);
the comparison of them with irrational animals (2 Pet. 2.12=Jude 10);
their revellings (2 Pet. 2.13=Jude 12); the mention of waterlessness
and the nether gloom of darkness (2 Pet. 2.17=Jude 13); the loud-
mouthed talking (2 Pet. 2.18=Jude 16). These references are all from
the second chapter of 2 Peter, but other parallels occur elsewhere:
e.g. 2 Pet. 1.12 with Jude 5; 2 Pet. 3.2f. with Jude 17f.; 2 Pet. 3.17
with Jude 24. They are noted at the appropriate places in the
commentary on 2 Peter.

The following list represents a more detailed comparison of the
main parallels between 2 Peter and Jude.

2 Peter	Jude
2.1–3. there will be false teachers among you, who will secretly bring in destructive heresies, even denying the Master who bought them . . . And many will follow	**4.** For admission has been secretly gained by some who long ago were designated for this condemnation, ungodly persons who pervert the grace of our God into

their licentiousness . . . from of old their condemnation has not been idle . . .

(With verse 3 cf. Jude 11 and 16.)

4. For if God did not spare the angels when they sinned, but cast them into hell and committed them to pits of nether gloom to be kept until the judgment.

6. if by turning the cities of Sodom and Gomorrah to ashes he condemned them to extinction and made them an example to those who were to be ungodly . . .

9f. to keep the unrighteous under punishment . . . and especially those who indulge in the lust of defiling passion and despise authority.

. . . are not afraid to revile the glorious ones, **11.** whereas angels . . . do not pronounce a reviling judgment upon them before the Lord.

12. But these, like irrational animals, . . . reviling in matters of which they are ignorant, will be destroyed in the same destruction with them.

13. They are blots and blemishes, revelling in their dissipation, carousing with you.

15. Forsaking the right way . . . they have followed the way of Balaam . . . who loved gain from wrongdoing . . .

licentiousness and deny our only Master . . .

6. And the angels that did not keep their own position . . . have been kept by him in eternal chains in the nether gloom until the judgment of the great day.

7. just as Sodom and Gomorrah and the surrounding cities, which likewise acted immorally . . . serve as an example by undergoing a punishment of eternal fire.

8. these men in their dreamings defile the flesh, reject authority and revile the glorious ones.

9. But when the archangel Michael, contending with the devil, disputed about the body of Moses, he did not presume to pronounce a reviling judgment upon him, but said, 'The Lord rebuke you.'

10. But these men revile whatever they do not understand, and by those things that they know by instinct as irrational animals do, they are destroyed.

12. These are blemishes on your love feasts, as they boldly carouse together . . .

11. For they walk in the way of Cain, and abandon themselves for the sake of gain to Balaam's error . . .

17. These are waterless springs and mists driven by a storm; for them the nether gloom of darkness has been reserved.	**12f.** These are . . . waterless clouds, carried along by winds; . . . for whom the nether gloom of darkness has been reserved for ever.
18. For, uttering loud boasts of folly, they entice with licentious passions of the flesh . . .	**16.** These are grumblers, malcontents, following their own passions, loud mouthed boasters, flattering people . . .
3.2. you should remember the predictions of the holy prophets and the commandment of the Lord and Saviour through your apostles.	**17.** you must remember, beloved (cf. 2 Pet. 3.1), the predictions of the apostles of our Lord Jesus Christ;
3. First of all you must understand this, that scoffers will come in the last days with scoffing, following their own passions . . .	**18.** they said to you, 'In the last time there will be scoffers, following their own ungodly passions.'

The correspondences between the two writings are too close to be a matter of accidental coincidence (though only once is a clause almost identical in both, namely 'for whom the nether gloom of darkness has been reserved [for ever]': 2 Pet. 2.17; Jude 13). Therefore one must be dependent on the other or both on a third source. The difficulty about direct borrowing is that the language is so similar yet often pointlessly different. But the postulate of a further document scarcely eases this. Perhaps the factor which would speak most strongly for the existence of a third source arises from the resemblance, pointed out by T. F. Glasson, between Jude 6, 2 Pet. 2.4, and a passage from Hesiod's account of the fight of Zeus against the Titans given in his *Theogony*. Zeus' supporters 'overshadowed the Titans with their missiles, and hurled them beneath the widespread earth, and bound them in bitter chains when they had conquered them by their strength for all their great spirits, as far beneath the earth as heaven is above earth; for so far is it from earth to Tartarus . . . There by the counsel of Zeus who drives the clouds the Titan gods are hidden under misty gloom, in a dank place where are the ends of the huge earth . . .'. (Translated by H. G. Evelyn White in the Loeb edition; quoted Glasson, *Greek Influence in Jewish Eschatology*, p. 63.) Jude 6 tells how 'the angels that did not keep their own position . . . have been kept by him in eternal chains in the nether gloom . . .' and 2 Pet. 2.4 says, 'God did not spare the angels when they sinned, but cast them into Tartarus and committed them to pits of nether gloom . . .' It is not impossible that Jude and 2 Peter should have connection with Hesiod; both show signs of Greek literary influence. Moreover, although the language involved could in principle have been derived from various places in 1 Enoch and the portions of the Book of Noah which Charles found embedded there, the same words occur *together* in Jude and 2 Peter as in Hesiod. But whereas Jude uses the same words as the Greek poet for 'chains' and 'gloom', 2 Peter uses the word for 'gloom' and makes a direct reference to 'Tartarus'. They appear to divide Hesiod's words between them. Again, 2 Pet. 2.17 alters Jude 13 to a remark about 'mists . . . for whom the nether gloom of darkness has been reserved'. But this again recalls confusedly the end of the Hesiod passage quoted above. Thus it might look as if both writers had access to the original of Hesiod or to another source which used it. But the notion of such a source is difficult, for so little of Jude does not reappear in 2 Peter that the hypothetical source must have been practically identical with it, so that it is hard to see why Jude should have reissued it with such minor alterations. But the possibility remains.

THE PRIORITY OF JUDE

Of the other two alternatives it is easier to imagine the author of 2 Peter condensing the references to angels and dropping the story from the *Assumption of Moses* in Jude 8ff. (see note *in loc.*) or the quotation from 1 Enoch in Jude 14f., than the other way round. Moreover, occasionally 2 Peter appears to recall the language of Jude but to use it in a different sense, as in the confused passages at 2 Pet. 2.12f. cf. Jude 10; 2 Pet. 2.17 cf. Jude 12f.; and the alteration of 'love-feasts' at Jude 12 to 'dissipation' in 2 Pet. 2.13 (*agapais* into *apatais* in Greek). It is also urged that it is hard to see why part of a letter issued in the name of Peter should be re-issued under the less

significant name of Jude, whoever he was. But this argument has
less force when it is remembered that the gnostics made great play
with the name of Jude-Didymus-Thomas as the Twin of our Lord,
and therefore his double; there was a brother of Jesus called Jude
(Mk 6.3) and the Aramaic name *Tōmā*, like the Greek Didymus,
means 'twin'. Therefore the names of the apostle Thomas Didymus
both mean 'twin', and he was identified with Jude as the Twin of
Jesus. Moreover the 'heresy' which it is the sole purpose of the
Epistle of Jude to combat represents a nascent gnosticism: how
appropriate then to issue it under this name. Moreover the 'James'
with whom the writer claims relationship is probably James the
Just, who himself figures as a hero of gnostic tradition.

Nevertheless, those who have maintained the priority of 2 Peter
have usually done so because they believed in its authenticity as a
work of the Apostle Peter. If this issue is temporarily set aside it is
immediately plausible in the light of the apparent signs of secondari-
ness noted above that 2 Peter should be a reissue of Jude expanded
to deal with the question of the delay of the End of the world.

If 2 Peter is dependent on Jude it is convenient to begin with the latter. The Epistle of Jude is a hortatory tract addressed to a Christian community or communities in some area which was in danger from subversive teaching and from subversive elements which had infiltrated into their own membership. The description of these elements is so vague as to make it difficult to tell whether a specific community is in view or not. The writer declares that he had intended to write in any case on the general topic of 'our common salvation' but now he has found that his specific object must be to exhort his readers to 'contend for the faith which was once for all delivered to the saints' (verse 3). The nature of the false teaching and the new behaviour is such as to convince the author that it is part of the trials preceding the End (see on verses 17f.) and that the troublemakers involved were destined from of old for their perverse role (verse 4). Their chief characteristics are insolence and libertinism; they despise authority, obey their animal instincts, wallow in ungodly passions and carousing (verses 8, 10, 18, 7, 12). They scoff at morality (verse 18), grumble at their lot (verse 16), and for gain ingratiate themselves (verses 16, 11). On the surface they are apparently malcontents stirring up trouble in the Christian community and introducing the more reprehensible Gentile practices. They resemble the people Paul had to deal with at Corinth. They are libertines (1 C. 5.1ff.; 6.12ff.; 10.8); they have visions and apparently take money for their revelations (Jude 8, 11, 16; cf. 2 C. 11.7; 12.1, 12; 1 C. 9.12, 14); they are loudmouthed and boastful (Jude 16; cf. 1 C. 4.7; 2 C. 5.12; 10.13, 12, 18); they claim to be 'spiritual' (Jude 19; cf. 2 C. 11.4); they turn the love-feasts into carousals (Jude 12; cf. 1 C. 11.20ff.). Jude has the same warning example as Paul (Jude 5; 1 C. 10.1ff.): the deliverance of Christ does not confer a dispensation to sin any more than did the deliverance from Egypt. Certain circumstances, however, suggest that the heretics with whom Jude was concerned had proceeded further than those at Corinth. They 'revile the glorious ones' (verse 8) by which is meant an order of angels, whereas Paul and other New Testament writers rather find the

worship of angels a danger. They evidently pander to the grosser
passions of people who are in a position to be of advantage to them,
and presumably by teaching them that such passions are not
unworthy of true religion (verse 16). But this is nearer to the
practices of the later heretics mentioned by such writers as Irenaeus
and Hippolytus and Epiphanius than the people who troubled
St Paul. Hippolytus tells of the followers of Simon Magus (i.e. the
sorcerer) who alleged the necessity of promiscuous intercourse,
saying, 'All earth is earth, and there is no difference where anyone
sows provided he does sow.' He wrote, 'They even congratulate
themselves on account of this indiscriminate intercourse, asserting
that this is perfect love, and employing the expressions, "holy of
holies" and "sanctify one another" ' (*Refut.* VI.14 A-N.C.L. translation). The followers of Carpocrates and others held that the world
was created by angels among whom was the God of the Jews, and
that they were enemies of the true God (Hippolytus, *op. cit.* VII.20;
Irenaeus, *Adv. Haer.* I.24f.). They held, in very modern vein, that
souls should have experience of every kind of life and every kind of
action, partly on the principle that the only way to liberation was to
work one's way through everything in a series of incarnations, and
partly on the principle that voluptuous sins were an affront to the
(evil) creator(s) of matter, and so show a true contempt for the
things of this world. When Jude speaks of those against whom his
letter is directed as 'worldly people devoid of the Spirit' (verse 19)
the word translated 'worldly people' (*psychikoi*) means those who
live a purely sensuous life; cf. 1 C. 2.14; 15.44; Jas 3.15. Gnostics
known to Irenaeus (I.6.2f.) held that the majority of Christians were
at the animal level, while they themselves were at the spiritual level
by nature. Jude seems to transfer this terminology to the heretics,
reversing the implications: the gnostics are the worldly, mere
animals (cf. verse 10) and 'devoid of the Spirit'. His advice to the
faithful is to build themselves up on the faith in which they have
been grounded (verse 20). They have need of the mercy of the Lord
Jesus Christ; they may fall from the love of God (verse 21). The
heretics neglect prayer, and feel no need of the Holy Spirit (verse 20,
cf. 19). Jude urges the faithful to have compassion on them, but
with great caution lest they catch the disease (verse 23). This last

verse, however, represents a traditional warning which appears also in the *Didache* (2.7).

1. LITERARY AFFINITIES

There are really no quotations from the Old Testament in the Epistle of Jude. The same chapter in Zechariah appears to furnish turns of phrase at different points; cf. the three contacts of Zech. 3.2, 4 with Jude 9, 23. When the author makes direct quotations he turns to the apocalyptic writings, and quotes from the so-called First Book of Enoch 1.9 in verses 13–15, beginning, 'Behold the Lord came' and ending 'spoken against him'. 'The seventh from Adam' in verse 13 is probably a quotation from a different part of the same book (60.8). The tale of the dispute between the devil and the archangel Michael over the body of Moses to which reference is made in verse 9 is taken, according to some of the Fathers, from *The Assumption of Moses* (see the note *in loc.*).

Jude is closely connected with 2 Peter, and, as indicated above, the latter incorporated it in his own work. This would seem to connect Jude with the Petrine circle, but the connection is not borne out by the use of apocalyptic sources. It may be held that there are reminiscences of 1 Enoch in 1 Peter, but 2 Peter ostentatiously avoids the direct citations made by Jude. It is not incongruous with Jude's apocalyptic affinity that some have detected a flavour of Greek poetry in the phrases of the epistle; later Jewish thought of all kinds was not unaffected by things Greek. Specific echoes have been found of Moschus, Euripides, and Hesiod (see on verse 13).

Jude shows definite acquaintance with Pauline terminology. He uses the word 'saints' for Christians, and 'called' in the same sense. 'Grace' appears in a Pauline sense when reference is being made to those who use God's kindness as an excuse for libertinism; see verse 4. When 2 Peter deals with the same problem (and even mentions Paul by name) he does not speak of 'grace' but of 'forbearance' (2 Pet. 3.15f.), though he uses the word 'grace' formally twice (1.2; 3.18, following the beginning and end of 1 Peter). Jude, in turning the heretics' use of the gnostic terminology of 'natural' and 'spiritual against them is, in fact, using the expressions in the same way as Paul does (see on verse 19).

There are similarities of language between Jude and the Pastoral Epistles, particularly in the way the word 'faith' is used for the Christian religion, in the use of the word 'remind', and the suggestion that Jude thought of 'godliness' as the norm of the Christian life rather than freedom or holiness or love (verses 4, 15, 18). On these words see below, pp. 77f. The semi-technical term 'deny' (verse 4) is a favourite with the author of the Pastorals, but appears also in the Johannine writings, the Synoptic Gospels, the Acts and Revelation. The salutation 'May mercy, peace, and love be multiplied to you' (verse 2) recalls 1 Pet. 1.1 but also *The Martyrdom of Polycarp* (mid-second century).

Whatever affinities there are between Jude and the Apostolic Fathers are explainable on the grounds of a similar use of language, and not of borrowing: e.g. the parallel with Jude 25 in 1 Clem. 20.12, 'to whom be glory and majesty', or Hermas, *Sim.* 5.7.2 with Jude 8, 'to defile the flesh'. The situation envisaged in the epistle was apparently sufficiently typical to explain the likeness (such as it is) between Jude 4f. and this from Barnabas 2.10: 'We ought, therefore, brethren, carefully to inquire concerning our salvation, in order that the evil one may not achieve a deceitful entry [a similar word to that used for 'admission has been secretly gained'] into us and hurl us away from our life' (translated by Lake in the Loeb series). The nearest parallel is in the *Didache* 2.7, 'Thou shalt hate no man; but some thou shalt reprove, and for some thou shalt pray, and some thou shalt love more than thine own life' (cf. Jude 23, and Barnabas 19.5, 'Thou shalt love thy neighbour more than thine own life'). Here traditional phraseology is probably behind the similarities.

2. DESTINATION

There is no indication of the destination of the Epistle of Jude. Some have thought that it could be connected with Egypt, because it is mentioned in the Muratorian Canon, was used by Clement of Alexandria and Origen, has parallels with the *Didache* (though there is no real evidence to pin this down to Egypt), and the fact that the

Carpocratian heresy (which has similarities with the heresy attacked in the epistle: see above, p. 71) originated there. Others find the home of the epistle in Syria (in which incidentally the *Didache* has also been located), where there was early much gnostic activity, including that concern with angels which is specifically mentioned (Jude 8f.). Streeter thought the writer was Bishop of Jerusalem early in the reign of the Emperor Trajan. Other suggested destinations have included Asia Minor and Corinth, because of the similarity of the trouble mentioned in St Paul's Corinthian correspondence. Destination and provenance are often closely connected by those who hold that the writer was familiar with conditions in a particular church. But if the letter is a general epistle, intended for the Church at large, the position becomes even more difficult. Certain features of the letter seem on the face of it to speak for a Jewish-Christian address, especially the use of extra-canonical Jewish apocalyptic writings. It is not impossible that gnosticism should infect a Jewish-Christian community; indeed Judaism has a close (and hitherto undetermined) connection with gnosticism, which makes great play with Hebrew words and names. Moreover, a connection between apocalyptic and gnosticism is by no means as bizarre as may appear at first sight: the two are undoubtedly connected at some points. For example, the two share a common outlook on the world and the flesh; apocalyptic played a great part in the later Jewish Kabbalistic mysticism; and the gnostics even wrote books called 'apocalypses', some of which have been preserved at Nag Hammadi (Chenoboskion). Doresse, *The Secret Books of the Egyptian Gnostics*, pp. 289f., has even tried to connect Qumran and the Dead Sea Covenanters with a new *Gospel of the Egyptians* found there. It alludes to the Apostle James the Great and mentions the 'Perfect', the seed of the great Seth, who dwell with him at Sodom and Gomorrah; and Doresse takes this to mean the Dead Sea district— perhaps, he says, Qumran was Gomorrah itself. It is remarkable that the Essenes lived in the district of Sodom. See on Jude 7. Probably, however, the mention of these cities is merely a reversing of Biblical values, as in the glorification of Cain among the Cainites (Irenaeus, *Adv. Haer.* I.31; see also Jude 11) who were probably Sethites. It is worth noting that the name 'Ophites' applied to these sectaries (and mentioned by some commentators in connection with Jude) was a blanket term used by the heresiologists to cover a variety of sects which did not call themselves by that name.

Jude is no doubt opposing the (earlier) apocalyptic to the (later) gnosticism. At the same time the use of apocalyptic sources is by no means an indication of Jewish provenance, in view of the popularity of this sort of writing among Christians.

3. EXTERNAL TESTIMONY

The Epistle of Jude occurs in the Muratorian Canon (late second century), is commented upon by Clement of Alexandria (*c.* 150–215), and is accepted by Tertullian (*c.* 160–220) and Origen (*c.* 185–254). Later it seems to have fallen into disrepute. Eusebius (*c.* 260–340), stressing the fact that it had little early recognition, placed it among the 'disputed' books, along with James and 2 Peter, and Jerome (*c.* 342–420) reported that many rejected it in his day because it quoted from the apocryphal 1 Enoch.

As we have seen, there is very little to connect the Epistle with the Apostolic Fathers, though even if a connection could be established it would not necessarily point only one way. Some have thought that Jude had a hand in the early Church Order called *The Didache* or *The Lord's Teaching to the Gentiles by the Twelve Apostles*; but the latter may be earlier, and either contributed phrases to Jude or (as is more likely) used similar traditional formulae. In any case the parallel to verse 23 is meagre (see comments *in loc.* and above, p. 73). The latter point applies to the resemblances to the second century *Martyrdom of Polycarp* (see on 2 and 25).

4. THE HERESY INVOLVED

Reason has been shown above and in the notes for the belief that the false teachers attacked by Jude were purveyors of an incipient gnosticism which denied the goodness of the created order and the necessity for observance of the moral law. They are in advance in these respects of the gnosticising movements mentioned elsewhere in the New Testament, and the lawless elements at Corinth which were a thorn in the side of St Paul. Their reference to the orthodox as 'psychical' (inferred from verse 19) and their contempt for angels (verses 8, 10 ?as creators of the world) with their practice of unnatural vice (verses 8, 23) in rebellion against authority place them in a different category. The fact that no specific destination seems to be implied in the Epistle, and the vagueness of the charges made, suggest that the heresy involved was comparatively widespread. We do not need, therefore, to indicate any special one, though those described by Hippolytus and Irenaeus in the passages cited above (p. 71) give a sufficient indication of what went on in antinomian gnostic circles. Doubtless there were early fringe sects of Judaism with strange doctrines, and the Judaism of the first century probably lent itself to this sort of thing more readily than is often supposed; but if the false teaching with which Jude is concerned was widespread (so that he need not be specific) and if it is of a different nature from that encountered in the early parts of the New Testament (which it is) then there is reason for believing that Jude belongs to the late strata of the canon. Christian Gnosticism, in fact, in any form that resembles the later full-blown heresy is a product of the second century.

5. USE OF PSEUDEPIGRAPHIC BOOKS AND THE STAGE OF DEVELOPMENT OF THE HERESY

Jude is peculiar in the New Testament in that he alone explicitly quotes a pseudepigraphic writing. This sets him aside from all the other contributors. But the significance of this fact is by no means unequivocal. Is it a sign that Jude is later than the others or earlier, or merely that he belonged to a section which treasured Enoch and the rest? The parts of the so-called First Book of Enoch utilized by Jude (for 1 Enoch is a composite work dated at various times) were written before the Christian era, so that this provides no *terminus a quo*. At the other end of the scale 1 Enoch and the other pseudepigrapha were popular among Christians until the third century; only then did they lose favour. 1 Enoch was used by 'Barnabas', Justin, Athenagoras, Tertullian, and Clement of Alexandria. Irenaeus knew of it but did not accept its version of the fall of the angels. Where the so-called *Epistle of Barnabas* was written (between 80 and 132)

1 Enoch was still regarded as inspired; 'Barnabas' cites it as Scripture. The vogue of the apocalypses was, however, waning in the second century. In sections of the Church and in Palestine, however, the process may have set in earlier. It has been suggested that in some circles at least speculation about Abraham was already replacing that upon Enoch in the latter part of the first century. This seems to be reflected in the Fourth Gospel and the first Epistle of John, which show acquaintance with the legends in *The Testament of Abraham* (see Sidebottom, *The Christ of the Fourth Gospel*, pp. 94f.). Among the Jews the fall of Jerusalem in 70 and finally the revolt of Bar Cochba in 132 put an end to the vogue of apocalyptic to which the rabbis (after 70) were particularly hostile. The same events may have affected Palestinian Christianity, and if Jude is a product of this it would set the upper limit of its composition at about the year 130. In point of fact, however, there is little evidence to connect Jude exclusively with Jewish-Christian circles. The use of pseudepigraphic works hardly counts, as we have just seen. But the so-called second Epistle of Peter utilized Jude extensively, while rejecting obvious quotations from these works. This suggests that the reaction had begun in the circles in which the two writers moved between the writing of Jude and the writing of 2 Peter.

More conclusive, in a region where even reasonable certainty is an impossibility, is the stage of development of the 'gnosticism' which Jude attacks. The probable year of the birth of Irenaeus is 130, and by his time gnosticism had crystallized into its various forms to an extent unknown in the New Testament. The relation between 2 Peter and Jude would therefore seem to suggest a date well before this for Jude, for there is still room for a great deal of development between 'Peter's' false teachers and those of Irenaeus. We can set the latest date for Jude then at, say, 120.

6. INTERNAL EVIDENCE

For the lower date it is necessary to depend exclusively upon the internal evidence of the epistle itself. The tone is that of the sub-apostolic age, closest in the New Testament to the Pastoral Epistles. The word 'remind' is typical of a time which looks back to the past

(2 Tim. 2.14; Tit. 3.1; 2 Pet. 1.12). 'The faith once delivered to the saints' (verse 3 and cf. 20) has a late ring; the life of those who are led by the Spirit of God (Rom. 8.14) has been codified and hardened into a rule of faith, an orthodoxy. Bigg, who believed that Jude was written early, yet said, 'his tone is that of a bishop of the fourth century'. Holiness is being replaced by piety ('godliness': verses 4, 15, 18). The heretics who are attacked in the letter 'defiled the flesh' presumably because they despised it in the fashion of the later gnostics. Jude shares their contempt for the flesh (verses 8, 23, 'hating even the garment spotted by the flesh'; cf. and contrast the passage that is echoed, i.e. Zech. 3.4, where there is no reference to the flesh). Besides all this, the 'predictions of the apostles of our Lord Jesus Christ' which refer to Jude's own time are placed in the relatively distant past: what they said was addressed to the readers indeed, but evidently they are no longer available to say it still (verse 17f.). What they said is to be remembered. At the earliest this suggests a date after the fall of Jerusalem in A.D. 70. This is the age of looking back to the origins of the Christian movement, the age when the faithful must be recalled to the sources of their faith. The date of the Pastoral Epistles is generally taken as between 100 and 120 with a preference for the later of these years. Jude would seem to be of about the same date. If, on the other hand, as de Zwaan, Jeremias, and Behm among others in recent years have maintained, the Pastorals are by Paul, then, of course, they must be considerably earlier, pre-64. This seems unlikely, and the evidence is largely of the kind which weighs in the case of Jude. The internal evidence of the Epistle of Jude therefore suggests a similar date to that indicated on other grounds, namely somewhat before 120.

7. AUTHORSHIP

The contents of the Epistle of Jude, apart from the salutation, give no indication of who the author was. The use of the apocalyptic pseudepigrapha does not prove that he was a Jew, for Christian writers used them freely until the third century; moreover there is nothing specially Jewish about the language and thought of the epistle. Verse 12 suggests that he was a countryman, but this need not be so either: the writer is indulging at this point in poetic elaboration and drawing on outside sources. The salutation claims that the Epistle is the work of 'Jude . . . the brother of James'. There are five men in the New Testament bearing the name of Jude or Judas who are associated with the Christian movement: (1) Judas Iscariot; (2) another of the apostles carefully distinguished from the former, the son (or perhaps the brother) of James (Lk. 6.16; Ac. 1.13; Jn 14.22) and apparently equivalent to Lebbaeus or Thaddaeus; (3) one of Jesus' four brothers (Mt. 13.55; Mk 6.3); (4) the man at Damascus with whom Paul lodged in the street called Straight after his conversion experience (Ac. 9.11); and (5) Judas surnamed Barsabbas, a leading figure in the church at Jerusalem (Ac. 15.22, 27, 32). Jude or Judas was, of course, a common name. The writer of the Epistle was certainly not the Apostle (2) with whom tradition confuses him, for he expressly dissociates himself from the apostles (verse 17). The fact that he calls himself 'brother of James' without qualification suggests that he was the third Judas above, brother of James the Great, bishop of Jerusalem and brother of the Lord, called James 'the Great' and 'the Just'. If this were the case, the date of the Epistle would have to be placed much earlier than that suggested above, say about 80. In support of this the argument is usually advanced that it is difficult to see why a forger or pseudepigraphist would assume the name of such an obscure figure as Jude. But, as we have already noted in the section on the relation between 2 Peter and Jude (pp. 68f., above), the name Jude was most appropriate at the head of a counterblast to gnosticism, which, later at least, made much of the notion that Jude was Jesus' twin, as well as claiming James the Just as one of its heroes (cf. Jude 1.1). The recently discovered *Gospel of Thomas* is, in fact, supposed to be by this person and begins, 'These are the secret words which the living Jesus spoke and Didymus Jude Thomas wrote'. As pointed out above, 'Didymus' and 'Thomas' both mean 'twin', so that 'Jude' is the only name that stands in its own right. This work was certainly in existence at the end of the second century and contains formulae as early as the middle of that century. It is quite possible, and from internal indications of date probable, that the Epistle of Jude is pseudonymous.

THE LETTER OF

JUDE

THE LETTER OF
JUDE

1 Jude, a servant of Jesus Christ and brother of James.

To those who are called, beloved in God the Father and kept for Jesus Christ:

2 May mercy, peace, and love be multiplied to you.

3 Beloved, being very eager to write to you of our common salvation, I found it necessary to write appealing to you to contend for the faith which was once for all delivered to the saints. 4 For admission has been secretly gained by some who long ago were designated for this condemnation, ungodly persons who pervert

---

THE SALUTATION 1–2

1. servant: see on Jas 1.1.

brother of James: see the Introduction above, p. 79.

those who are called: cf. Mt. 22.14; Rom. 1.6f.; 8.28; 1 C. 1.2, 24; Rev. 17.14; also Jn 15.16 and 1.13. A technical term for 'Christians' implying that they are chosen and appointed and invited by God. The word is Pauline; it does not occur in either of the Petrine epistles. The same is true of 'saints' (verse 3), 'worldly people' (*psychikoi*) and 'spirit' (verse 19).

beloved in God: a curious phrase, perhaps meaning 'beloved as far as God is concerned', cf. 1 C. 14.11, 'the speaker will be a foreigner to me (lit., *in* me)'. There is no New Testament phrase 'in God' equivalent to the Pauline 'in Christ'. Hort declared that the whole phrase 'is without analogy, and admits no natural interpretation'. He thought the 'in' was intended to stand before 'Jesus Christ'. But an approach is made in the Johannine sayings 'Beloved, if God so loved us, we also ought to love one another' and 'God is love, and he who abides in love abides in God, and God abides in him' (1 Jn 4.11, 16). Cf. with this Jude 21.

kept: cf. verse 6 and 1 Th. 5.23; Rev. 3.10. The word occurs five times in Jude: in verses 1, 6 (*bis*), 13, 21. Perhaps 'kept in store' for the second coming (cf. 21), but more probably 'kept from the world' (cf. 1 Jn 5.18).

for Jesus Christ: or 'by Jesus Christ', as implied in Jn 5.18.

2. mercy, peace, and love: the expression is close to the sub-apostolic formula 'grace, mercy, peace' (1 Tim. 1.2; 2 Tim. 1.2; Tit. 1.4; 2 Jn 3; but cf. Gal. 6.16). Love, grace, and mercy are much more closely connected in meaning than appears from the English translation. Love is what impels one towards another; in Christian parlance the impetus of the goodness of God overflowing into the lives of men. Peace is the characteristic Christian experience and the greeting implies more than the Old Testament wish for prosperity, though this itself springs from the unstinting goodwill of God: bliss in mind and soul is intended.

be multiplied to you: a Semitic expression; cf. Dan. 4.1, 'Peace be multiplied to you' and 1 Pet. 1.2. The same expression 'mercy, peace, and love . . . be multiplied' is used in the salutation of *The Martyrdom of Polycarp* (mid-second century).

THE INTENTION OF THE LETTER 3-17

INFILTRATION OF SUBVERSIVE ELEMENTS 3, 4

3. Beloved: another conventional term, used in the New Testament much as in later liturgical forms of address to the congregation. It is difficult to tell from the content of the epistle whether Jude is writing to a specific community, to the churches in a particular area, or to Christians in general.

being very eager to write . . . found it necessary: Jude was anxious to write more generally, but circumstances force upon him a more limited task.

contend: a very strong word: 'strive urgently'.

the faith . . . once for all delivered: a dogmatic formula, with a late flavour; cf. 17, where the apostolic age is past. Jude manages another reference to 'your most holy faith' in his short epistle (verse 20). 'The faith' occasionally has something of this meaning in Paul (cf. Gal. 1.23); but nowhere clearly the sense (as here) of a body of doctrine and practice laid down once for all.

saints: Christians, as those holy to God and by contact with him in Christ. The term is typical of Paul.

4. admission has been secretly gained by some: not only is the local community troubled by importations of an alien creed, but it seems that the heretics themselves have invaded the church, bringing their doctrines with them. Paul had experience of such: 2 C. 11.4.

long ago were designated: perhaps a reference to Old Testament prophecies, or to the notion of one's destiny being written in heaven; cf. 1 Enoch 108.7 ('Fragment of the Book of Noah'): 'For some of them are written and inscribed above in the heaven, in order that the angels may read them and how that which shall befall the sinners, and the spirits of the humble, etc.'. Jude quotes Enoch later (verse 14) and refers to the Enochic doctrine of angels (verse 6). Enoch himself according to one account ascended to become the recording angel Metatron. For the doctrine in the rabbis, see *Esther Rab.* 82a. Cf. also Dan. 7.10; Rev. 20.12; CD 2.6f. Lk. 10.20 uses the same figure.

for this condemnation: lit., judgment. The implication is that the judgment and the sin are one (cf. the past tense in verse 11); the heretics were foreordained to their sorry function as ungodly persons who creep in and pervert the grace of God into licentiousness, and deny our only Master and Lord, Jesus Christ.

ungodly persons: impious. The word is connected with antinomianism (see

the grace of our God into licentiousness and deny our only Master and Lord, Jesus Christ.

5 Now I desire to remind you, though you were once for all fully

---

below) in 1 Tim. 1.9, and in the *Assumption of Moses* 7.1 with those who shall be when 'the times are ended': cf. Jude 18; 1 Jn 2.18. The word is, however, quite conventional for the ungodly in general.

who pervert the grace of our God into licentiousness: in Rom. 3.8; 6.1, 15, Paul contends against the view that 'being under grace' allows Christians to do evil with impunity. The view that it does (called historically ' antinomianism') has cropped up at various times in the Church. In the early years it was associated with one wing of the gnostic movement. A basic tenet of gnosticism was that the material world and the flesh were evil and therefore gnostics took one of two contradictory views: either it was necessary to practise asceticism and mortify the flesh, or the deeds done by the body did not count and licence was harmless.

and deny . . . Jesus Christ: Jesus, or perhaps God the Father (cf. Tit. 1.16), is the **Master** to whom we are 'enslaved'. 'Deny' is practically a technical term in the New Testament. Debauchery is a denial of him who (in Jewish terms) is the way as well as the life and the truth. The classic argument against antinomianism is 1 Jn 3.1ff., e.g., 'You know that he appeared to take away sin . . . Let no one deceive you. He who does right is righteous as he is righteous. He who commits sin is of the devil, for the devil has sinned from the beginning. The reason the Son of God appeared was to destroy the works of the devil. No one born of God commits sin, for God's nature abides in him'. That is, religious right-doing is recognizable as morality; it is the nature of God to be good, and those who take their life from him are good in the same way: 'Whoever does not do right is not of God, nor he who does not love his brother' (1 Jn 3.10). This is a chief lesson of the Old Testament.

More may be implied, as when 2 Jn 7 says, 'Many deceivers have gone out into the world, men who will not acknowledge the coming of Jesus Christ in the flesh; such a one is the deceiver and the antichrist' (cf. 1 Jn 2.22ff.) Gnostics denied a true incarnation because of their low view of the flesh. They also separated the Creator God from the Redeemer, declaring that the former was evil, as the source of matter, the evil principle. Perhaps the author of 1 Jn 2.22f. has this in mind when he writes, 'This is the antichrist, he who denies the Father and the Son. No one who denies the Son has the Father. He who confesses the Son has the Father also'. Denying Christ is rejecting him as a true revelation of God, the God who is the Creator and source of all that is.

NO ONE IS SECURE IN THE FAVOUR OF GOD IF HE PRESUMES UPON IT 5–7

5. remind: typical in sub-apostolic literature: 2 Tim. 2.14; Tit. 3.1; 2 Pet. 1.12. **once for all fully informed:** lit., once for all *knew*. The addressees of the epistle

informed, that he who saved a people out of the land of Egypt,
afterward destroyed those who did not believe. ⁶ And the angels
that did not keep their own position but left their proper dwelling

---

have fallen away from their former convictions (cf. Gal. 1.6). The early Church
carefully instructed converts (cf. Lk. 1.4). Some MSS place the 'once for all' in the
next clause. The word *hapax* need mean merely 'once': cf. 2 C. 11.25, 'once I
was stoned'. This is likely here: 'The Lord saved once . . . the second time' (*RSV*
'afterward'). *Hapax* does not mean 'for the first time' and perhaps a copyist has
corrected the grammar by transferring it to the previous clause. This verse abounds
in emendations.

he who saved . . . afterward destroyed: The *RSV* translation represents a
conjecture of Westcott and Hort: the MSS have " 'Jesus', 'the Lord' or 'God'
saved". (See *RSV* margin. The *NEB* notes that Jesus might be understood here
as 'Joshua'.) The New Testament teaching of the goodness of God (cf. Jas 1.17
and note there; also Paul *passim* on the 'grace' of God) was liable to the miscon-
struction that no retribution would fall on the sinner. Jude insists that the Saviour
can also be the Destroyer. Paul did not attack the problem of antinomianism
from this angle; he argued not from the fact that there would be punishment for
sin but that sin in a life in Christ was intolerable morally (cf. Rom. 6.1f., 19f.);
1 C. 6.15 ('Shall I take the members of Christ and make them members of a pros-
titute? Never!'). Nor is Jude sensitive to the problem raised by the notion of a
personal wrath of God in the light of God's moral consistency. For **afterward**
(lit., a second time), see above. The incident of the destruction of the unbelieving
Israelites is used for warning in 1 C. 10.5; Heb. 4.7f.; Ps. 95.7f. (cf. Num. 14.11;
Dt. 1.32).

who did not believe: here belief involves obedience.

6. And the angels: becoming 'spiritual' (verse 19, where Jude turns the language
of the gnostics against themselves) does not absolve men from morality. Even
angels (the most spiritual of beings) were punished when they disobeyed. But the
angels evidently come to mind because the heretics reviled them: verse 8.

did not keep their proper position: lit., rule, domain. This is not the doctrine
that the angels fell because of pride (so, e.g., Origen) but that they became a prey
to fleshly lust. They did not seek to rise higher but to fall lower (cf. Justin, 1 *Apol.*
2.5). Jude cannot therefore intend this as a warning against usurping authority
(verse 8) so much as against defiling the flesh (*ibid*). The legend of the angels who
married the comely daughters of men and begot children by them is first stated
in Gen. 6.1–4, and is expanded in 1 Enoch 6ff. See also Jubil. 5.1ff.; 2 Baruch 56.12f.
The story is repeated elsewhere: e.g., Philo, Josephus, *The Testaments of the Twelve
Patriarchs*, *Genesis Rabba*, and throughout 1 Enoch. Similar stories of marriages
between heavenly beings and men occur in Greek sources, in which they are also
connected with a Flood as in Enoch, which turns the incidental connection in

7

have been kept by him in eternal chains in the nether gloom until
the judgment of the great day; ⁷ just as Sodom and Gomor'rah and
the surrounding cities, which likewise acted immorally and indulged in unnatural lust, serve as an example by undergoing a
punishment of eternal fire.

8 Yet in like manner these men in their dreamings defile the flesh,

---

Genesis into a causal one. The language of Jude and 2 Pet. 2.4 show resemblances
to that of Hesiod's account of the punishment of the Titans (see Introduction,
pp. 67f., and below).

**kept by him in eternal chains in the nether gloom until the judgment of
the great day:** cf. 1 Enoch 10.12f.: 'Bind them fast for seventy generations in the
valleys of the earth, till the day of their judgment'. This concerns the angels, but
cf. 1 Enoch 22.11: 'Here their spirits [i.e., this time of the dead] shall be set apart
in this great pain till the great day of judgment . . . There he shall bind them for
ever . . .;' cf. also 1 Enoch 11.12; 12.4. Hesiod (*Theogony*) in his description of
Zeus' punishment of the Titans uses the same words as Jude for 'chains' and
'gloom' (see above, Introduction, p. 68). But note that in 1 Enoch 10.4 Azazel is
to be cast into *darkness* cf. 54.4).

the great day: cf. 1 Enoch 54.6, 'And Michael and Gabriel and Raphael and
Phanuel shall take hold of them on that great day and cast them into the burning
furnace.'

7. Sodom and Gomorrah: Gen. 19. The classic Jewish example of immorality,
used also in 1 Clem. 11.1. Angels were also involved, in that the male population
wished to ravish two of them. Irenaeus (*Adv. Haer.* I.31) mentions the Cainites
(cf. Jude 11) whom others identify with the Ophites or Sethites and says that they
believe Cain to derive his being from the Power above, and claim kinship with
Esau, Korah, and the Sodomites. For other Sethites, Sodom and Gomorrah were
the abode of the perfect seed of the Great Seth (see Introduction above, p. 74).

likewise acted immorally: i.e., like the angels. These did not, of course, commit
sodomy, i.e., homosexual acts; but Jude, like his mentor the author of 1 Enoch,
tends to despise all sexual activity: cf. 8 and 23 ('hating even the garment spotted
by the flesh'). See 1 Enoch 12.4, 'the Watchers of heaven who have left the high
heaven, the holy eternal place, and have defiled themselves with women, and have
done as the children of earth do, and have taken unto themselves wives'. Jude
shares with the gnostics their low view of the flesh.

surrounding cities: Zoar, Admah, and Zeboim (Gen. 19.22; Dt. 29.23; Hos.
11.8). Zoar, at the southern end of the Dead Sea, survived.

indulged in unnatural lust: lit., 'going away after different flesh', which could
refer equally to the Sodomites lusting after the angels and the angels lusting after
earthly women.

example: the Greek word is used only here in the New Testament. The meaning is that the destruction of Sodom and Gomorrah was a warning to all men as the punishment of the angels was 'a testimony to the kings and mighty who possess the earth' (1 Enoch 67.12).

punishment of eternal fire: cf. Mt. 5.22; 13.42, 50; 18.8; 25.41; Rev. 20.14f. The volcanic nature of the Dead Sea area and the Gehenna gorge seemed to the Jews to be a permanent result of the destruction of Sodom and the other cities by fire, which continued to burn underground. Cf. Wis. 10.7, 'to whose wickedness a smoking waste still witnesses, and plants bearing fair fruit that comes not to ripeness'. Josephus, (*Wars of the Jews*, IV.8.4), tells of the remains of the fire, and later Tertullian (*Apol.* 40), wrote that the fruit of the trees fell to ashes at the touch. For the combination of darkness and fire see 1QS 2.8, 'the gloom of eternal fire'.

DESCRIPTION OF THE HERETICS 8-16

8. in like manner these men: i.e., the heretics, who despise all authority, moral or otherwise. The illustrations of the Watchers and the men of Sodom have been chosen evidently because the heretics reviled angels, and because of the vice involved, though this verse really only presupposes the second illustration. If they were also men like the Sethites who reversed ordinary concepts and made Sodom and Gomorrah the home of the Perfect (see above), the latter illustration would be more apt than appears at first sight.

in their dreamings: to 'dream dreams' is to have visions in dreams: Ac. 2.17 (Jl 3.1) and the noun in Homer (*Odyssey* XIV.495). The heretics take money for their revelations (verses 11, 16); cf. 1 C. 9; 2 C. 12.13-16 where Paul claims that he was no burden on the congregation; but the position is different.

defile the flesh: Jude connects this directly with the dreaming, perhaps in bitter irony (cf. 23). Paul's opponents indulged in sexual licence (1 C. 5.1ff.; 6.12ff.; 10.8; 2 C. 12.21), as did the later gnostics, such as the Carpocratians and Marcosians and the followers of Simon Magus. Hippolytus, *Refut.* VII.20; VI.14; Irenaeus, *Adv. Haer.* I.25, 23, 13ff. According to Hippolytus, *Refut.* VI.14, the followers of Simon referred to promiscuous intercourse as 'perfect love' and insisted that, since 'all earth is earth', 'it matters not where one sows the seed so long as it is sown'. We still know so little at first hand of gnosticism that it is impossible to tell whether or not these practices were symbolic rituals (e.g., expressive of the gathering in of the seed of light scattered among all men) or orgies carried out in contempt of the physical nature created by an evil god, or mere licentiousness or even calumnies of the heresiologists.

reject authority: lit., 'lordship'. Possibly this refers to the tendency of a nascent gnosticism to reject the authority of the creator god. It would combine with a rejection of all authority, both in the Church and in the moral order. The fact that the word is in the singular in the best texts makes the reference to angelic powers unlikely; but no explanation is really satisfactory (cf. also Heb. 13.9, 7, 17).

reject authority, and revile the glorious ones. ⁹ But when the archangel Michael, contending with the devil, disputed about the body
of Moses, he did not presume to pronounce a reviling judgment
upon him, but said, 'The Lord rebuke you.' ¹⁰ But these men revile
whatever they do not understand, and by those things that they
know by instinct as irrational animals do, they are destroyed.
¹¹ Woe to them! For they walk in the way of Cain, and abandon

---

revile the glorious ones: the order of angels known as 'glories' (literal translation) is evidently referred to. This concern for the honour of angels is unusual
in the New Testament where worship of angels is usually the danger (Col. 2.18;
Rev. 19.10; 22.8f.). But, once again, if the beliefs of the later sects are any guide,
here is another feature of the gnosticism which despises angels as agents of creation
or perhaps as rulers of fate whom Christ outwitted (cf. perhaps verse 16 where the
word rendered 'malcontents' means, literally, complaining of one's lot, and
1 C. 2.8).

9. the archangel Michael: cf. Dan. 10.13, 21; 12.1; Rev. 12.7.

contending with the devil: cf. Rev. 12.7.

disputed about the body of Moses: the reference is to a Jewish tradition contained, according to Clement of Alexandria (*Adumb. in Ep. Judae*), Origen (*de
Princ.* iii.2.1) and Didymus, in the *Assumption of Moses* (a part which has not come
down to us). It told that when Moses died (of the kiss of God) a contention arose
between Michael and the devil over the body. The latter claimed it on the ground
that he was lord of the material order, and, on being confronted by Michael with
the proposition that all creation is God's, shifted his ground and declared that
Moses as a murderer (Exod. 2.12) was not worthy of burial at all.

did not presume . . . reviling judgment upon him: presumably because the
devil was an angel, though fallen, and still one of the 'authorities'.

'The Lord rebuke you': the words of the angel to Satan in Zech. 3.2. This
chapter is quoted several times in Jude: see also verses 22 and 23.

10. But these men revile whatever they do not understand: claiming
superior knowledge they yet show a lack of respect for the denizens of the spiritual
world which the archangel would not show to the devil.

by those things they know by instinct . . . they are destroyed: this is
vituperation pure and simple. The heretics know nothing but what their animal
instincts teach them and these lead to destruction: cf. Phil. 3.18f., '. . . enemies of
the cross of Christ. Their end is destruction, their god is the belly, and they glory
in their shame, with minds set on earthly things'.

11. Woe to: i.e., also for! Used only here, at 1 C. 9.16 and in Revelation
outside the Gospels. It represents the introduction to a prophetic lament (or taunt-
song).

themselves for the sake of gain to Balaam's error, and perish in Korah's rebellion. ¹² These are blemishes on your love feasts, as they boldly carouse together, looking after themselves; waterless clouds, carried along by winds; fruitless trees in late autumn, twice

---

Cain . . . Balaam . . . Korah: Cain appears as the murderer (and so the man of unrighteousness) *par excellence* in the Book of Wisdom (10.3), 1 Enoch, *The Testament of Abraham*, and the first epistle of John (3.12). He is the type of the cynical worldling in Philo and the Jerusalem Targum. For Balaam see Num. 22–24; 31.16; Jos. 24.9f.; Mic. 6.5; Rev. 2.14; cf. Num. 22.18; *Aboth* 5.29. (The sect of the Nicolaitans mentioned in connection with Balaam in the Revelation passage reminds one of Jude's troublemakers.) Cain was represented in one tradition as a false teacher leading the Israelites into licentiousness for gain. So did the heretics (and cf. 1 Tim. 6.5). He had dreams and visions and ignored an angel. Korah (Num. 16) and his friends rebelled against Moses, for which they were buried alive, and, according to R. Akiba (*Sanh.* 10.3) have no part in the world to come. Korah is not mentioned elsewhere in the New Testament. He and Cain, along with the Sodomites, were held in reverence by the Sethites called Cainites by Irenaeus. But Epiphanius has a note about such a sect that believed in angels who blinded Moses and resurrected Korah and his group. These myths seem to have been held in common by groups distinguished only by the originality of their leaders.

12. **blemishes:** the word for 'reefs' is identical in form (yet a third word of the same form means a 'squall' or 'storm'), but 'blemishes' seem appropriate here. 'Dirty persons' is also possible.

love feasts: some MSS read 'dissipation' as in 2 Pet. 2.13. This makes little sense. The love-feast was the common meal eaten by the early Christians in connection with the Eucharist (cf. 1 C. 11.20ff). It is mentioned only here and (possibly) at 2 Pet. 2.13 in the New Testament. The *Didache* (11.9) gives the injunction that no prophet who orders a meal 'in the spirit' is to eat of it, or else he is not a true prophet. This is not the same thing, but it recalls 11 and 16.

boldly: lit., 'without fear'. They were irreverent, shameless.

looking after themselves: lit., 'shepherding themselves': a reference to Ezek. 34.2, 8, 10, where the unworthy shepherds look after themselves and not the sheep. For similar behaviour see 1 C. 11.21f.

waterless clouds, carried along by winds: i.e., shedding no useful rain.

fruitless trees in late autumn: i.e., almost in winter; but possibly trees which are fruitless when fruit is expected, namely in autumn.

twice dead, uprooted: in Rev. 20.14 the 'second death' is the end prepared for all associates of the devil. Perhaps Jude thinks this fate has overtaken these men proleptically. But he is drawing out the analogy of the trees and heaping up the dead, uprooted; ¹³ wild waves of the sea, casting up the foam of their own shame; wandering stars for whom the nether gloom of darkness has been reserved for ever.

14 It was of these also that Enoch in the seventh generation from Adam prophesied, saying, 'Behold, the Lord came with his holy myriads, ¹⁵ to execute judgment on all, and to convict all the ungodly of all their deeds of ungodliness which they have committed in such an ungodly way, and of all the harsh things which ungodly sinners have spoken against him.' ¹⁶ These are grumblers, mal-

---

details: they are not only dead but doubly dead because uprooted (cf. also Heb. 10.29).

13. wild waves of the sea . . . their own shame: cf. Isa. 57.20. Bigg sees reminiscences of Greek poetry, quoting Moschus, *Idyll* 5.5; and Euripides, *Herc. Fur.* 851.

wandering stars for whom the nether gloom of darkness has been reserved for ever: the planets who transgressed and were punished are mentioned in 1 Enoch 18.13ff.; 21.1ff.; 90.24. But the stars were punished in fire, though the apocalyptists had no difficulty in combining fire and darkness (see on 7 above); this verse in Jude is an echo of verse 6 above. Here again is poetic language. This clause is the only one shared almost wholly by Jude and 2 Peter, despite the close resemblance of the two works in matter, form and turns of phrase.

THE PROPHECY OF ENOCH 14–16

14. of these: lit., 'to these'; Jude has some odd uses of the dative.

seventh . . . from Adam: cf. 1 Enoch 60.8.

'Behold, the Lord came . . . spoken against him': (end of verse 15): a direct quotation from 1 Enoch 1.9. In Jude the original is telescoped so that 'to destroy the ungodly and convict all flesh' becomes 'convict all the ungodly'. There is no reference to the Messiah in the opening chapters of 1 Enoch: it is God who comes. Jude might have thought of the Second Coming of Christ.

myriads: lit., tens of thousands. The holy myriads are angels (cf. Dt. 33.2; Zech. 14.5; Dan. 4.13; 8.13). The expression is common throughout 1 Enoch. The quotation from Enoch was proof to many in Jerome's time that the epistle of Jude was not inspired scripture. To Clement of Alexandria and Tertullian at an earlier date the reverse was true: Jude's quotation proved the inspiration of 'Enoch'.

15. to execute judgment: the same expression as in Jn 5.27, where, however, the background is probably Wis. 9.3 (cf. Wis. 9.1f. and Eph. 4.24) together with Dan. 7.13.

16. grumblers: the word does not appear elsewhere in the New Testament. In

contents, following their own passions, loud-mouthed boasters, flattering people to gain advantage.

17 But you must remember, beloved, the predictions of the apostles of our Lord Jesus Christ; [18] they said to you, 'In the last time there will be scoffers, following their own ungodly passions.'

---

the LXX the grumblers are those who complained against God in the wilderness: Exod. 15.24; 17.3; Num. 14.29. The verse echoes several passages in the *Assumption of Moses* (7.7, 9; 5.5).

malcontents: again the only occurrence in the New Testament: literally, those who complain against their lot. But the word is found in the sense of 'censorious', or simply as the opposite of 'blameless'. Presumably here it refers to the complaints of the heretics against God, against the celestial powers, and against authority in general. The equivalent word in the *Assumption of Moses* is *querulosi*.

loud-mouthed boasters: lit., their mouth 'talks big'. The parallel to the verse from 'following their own passions' to 'loud-mouthed boasters' in the *Assumption of Moses* 7.9 reads, 'et manus eorum et mentes eorum immunda tractantes, et os eorum loquitur ingentia'.

flattering people: lit., admiring faces. The expression does not appear elsewhere in the New Testament. It is the equivalent of the Semitic expression to 'take the face', in Hebrew, *nāsā' pānîm*, i.e., show favouritism: in the LXX at Gen. 19.21; Dt. 10.17; 2 Chr. 19.7; cf. Lev. 19.15; Mk 12.14 and Jas 2.1–9. The heretics court the favour of the influential, flattering people to gain advantage. The parallel passage in the *Assumption of Moses* (5.5) is 'mirentes personas cupiditatum et accipientes munera'.

PREDICTIONS OF THE APOSTLES AND EXHORTATIONS
TO HOLD THE FAITH 17–23

17. But you: emphatic in contradistinction to **these** at the beginning of verse 16. **predictions:** lit., 'things said beforehand'. Since these things referred to what was already happening in Jude's time, the predictions are placed in the relatively distant past.

the apostles: Jude thus distinguishes himself from the apostles: '*they* said to you' (next verse).

18. they said to you: the following words are printed by the *RSV* in quotation marks, but they are not necessarily a quotation. Such predictions seem to have sprung from a common feeling in the later apostolic age (cf. Ac. 20.29f.; 1 Tim. 4.1ff.; 2 Tim. 3.1ff.).

In the last time, etc.: the coming of Christ had convinced his followers that the present age was nearing its end. They believed that the signs of this were a falling

¹⁹ It is these who set up divisions, worldly people, devoid of the Spirit. ²⁰ But you, beloved, build yourselves up on your most holy faith; pray in the Holy Spirit; ²¹ keep yourselves in the love of God; wait for the mercy of our Lord Jesus Christ unto eternal life. ²² And convince some, who doubt; ²³ save some, by snatching them out of

---

off of standards, an increase of scepticism and licence: 'scoffers, following their own ungodly passions'. Cf. 1 Jn 2.17f.: 'And the world passes away, and the lust of it . . . Children, it is the last hour . . .'; also 2 Th. 2.3ff., and the general warnings against false teachers in Mk 13.5; Mt. 7.15.

scoffers: those who scoff at authority, particularly that of the moral order.

19. these who set up divisions: The word only occurs here in the New Testament. False beliefs produced cliques; the troublemakers ingratiated themselves with the rich (verses 11, 16). Later gnosticism influenced the educated class.

worldly people, devoid of the Spirit: the word translated 'worldly people' (*psychikoi*) means those who live a purely sensuous existence (cf. 1 C. 2.14; 15.44; Jas 3.15). The gnostics known to Irenaeus (I.6.2f.) held that church-people in general were purely animal who needed good works to be saved, while they themselves were saved anyhow because they were spiritual by nature. Thus various of them did not scruple to eat meat offered to idols, or to attend the gladiatorial games, or to seduce women. Jude apparently transfers this terminology to the gnostics themselves (cf. verse 10).

20. build yourselves up: cf. Eph. 2.19ff.

your most holy faith: i.e., the teaching of the Church: cf. verse 3.

pray in the Holy Spirit: cf. Rom. 8.26; Eph. 6.18.

21. keep yourselves in the love of God: again there is a parallel with Ephesians, this time at Eph. 3.17. 'Keep' is a favourite word with Jude: see verses 1, 6 (*bis*), 13, 21 and cf. Jn 15.9f., 'Abide in my love. If you keep my commandments you will abide in my love, just as I have kept my Father's commandments and abide in his love.'

wait for the mercy . . . unto eternal life: the judgment is coming on the ungodly (verse 14f.); mercy and eternal life are in store for the pious. 'Unto eternal life' is quite probably to be connected with 'keep yourselves' above: 'keep yourselves in the love of God . . . for eternal life' (the intervening words constitute a participial phrase in Greek).

22. convince some: the pious are not to be concerned merely with themselves. The implication that only 'some' are capable of salvation is not essential if this sentence is a conventional one, as the parallel in the *Didache* suggests (see below). Other MSS read 'have mercy on' for 'convince'. Yet others reduce the three clauses to two by omitting certain words, but this produces anomalous grammatical assumptions. Yet the original sentence may have had only two clauses, since

the fire; on some have mercy with fear, hating even the garment
spotted by the flesh.

24 Now to him who is able to keep you from falling and to
present you without blemish before the presence of his glory with

---

there seem to be only two classes of people in question, not three: e.g., 'Pity some
who doubt (or, convince those who dispute), and save others as snatching them
from the fire'. The whole sentence is evidently upset by some scribal error. Some
think it should read (with the Philoxenian Syriac, the Sahidic Coptic, Clement of
Alexandria, and Jerome), 'Snatch some from the fire; have mercy on them when
they repent (or, waver, i.e., doubt)'.

who doubt: i.e., waver; or, possibly, dispute.

23. snatching them from the fire: cf. Zech. 3.2 and Jude 9 and later in this
verse, where echoes of this Zechariah passage seem to be discernible.

have mercy with fear: *sc.* of contamination. Mercy must not become a snare
luring the orthodox into the falsehood of those he is trying to help.

The parallel in the *Didache* 2.7 is as follows: 'Thou shalt hate no man; but some
thou shalt reprove, and for some thou shalt pray, and some thou shalt love more
than thine own life' (cf. the similar form in *Barnabas* 19.5). The *Didache* (probably
much earlier than Jude) omits reference to contamination: evidently a different
situation is envisaged.

hating even the garment spotted by the flesh: probably another reminiscence
of Zech. 3, this time of verse 4. The expression is, however, a curious one, not
wholly explained by this, because the Old Testament passage has no mention of
'the flesh'. The verse has overtones of that late horror of the flesh which was the
chief influence in gnostic belief and also infected the orthodox. The **garment** (tunic
or shirt) was worn next to the skin. *The Gospel of the Egyptians* (Clement of Alexandria, *Stromateis* III.92.2) speaks of 'treading on the garment of shame'; cf.
The Gospel of Thomas, log. 37. 'His disciples said, "When will you be revealed
to us, and when will we see you?" Jesus said, "When you take off your clothes
without being ashamed, and take your clothes and put them under your feet
like little children and tread on them, then you will see the Son [or, you will
become sons] of the Living One and will not fear" ': cf. Oxyr. Papyrus 655. 42.

DOXOLOGY 24–25

24. to him who is able: the third doxology in the New Testament which so
begins (cf. Rom. 16.25; Eph. 3.20); the former of which has other resemblances
(see below).

keep you from falling: i.e., guard you from stumbling and keep you surefooted,
used equally of a horse or a man's moral equilibrium.

present you: lit., 'make you stand' but not in reference to falling: cf. Col. 1.22,

rejoicing, **25** to the only God, our Saviour through Jesus Christ our Lord, be glory, majesty, dominion, and authority, before all time and now and for ever. Amen.

'in order to present you holy and blameless and irreproachable before him'. The language of the doxology is appropriate to the subject of the epistle but is conventional and not necessarily framed with the previous warnings in view.

before the presence of his glory is a conventional Hebrew reverential periphrasis for 'in his presence'.

25. to the only God: cf. Rom. 16.27 'to the only wise God', from whence some MSS add the word 'wise' here and in 1 Tim. 1.17. The expression may mean 'to God only' (cf. also 1 Tim. 1.17; 6.15f., and Jn 5.44).

our Saviour through Jesus Christ is an unlikely punctuation. The phrase should more probably read, 'to the only God our Saviour, through Jesus Christ, etc.'. God the Father is called 'Saviour' eight times in the New Testament, six being in the Pastoral Epistles and one here: 1 Tim. 1.1; 2.3; 4.10; Tit. 1.3; 2.10; 3.4. The other is in the Hebraistic early chapters of Luke (1.47, cf. 2.11). It is more frequently used of Christ, and most frequently in the Pastoral Epistles and 2 Peter.

through Jesus Christ our Lord is omitted by late MSS and in the New Testament is only found in doxologies here and at Rom. 16.27 (cf. 1 Pet. 4.11).

before all time: also omitted by late MSS: lit., 'before the age.' There is some confusion over the whole phrase **before all time and now and for ever. Amen** in the MS tradition.

No doubt liturgical influence has been at work. No other doxology in the New Testament is so like later usage. Cf. Rom. 9.5; 16.27; 1 Pet. 4.11; Eph. 3.21. Here, as at the beginning, there is a parallel in the *Martyrdom of Polycarp* XX: 'to him who is able to bring us all in his grace and bounty to his heavenly kingdom through his only-begotten child Jesus Christ, be glory, honour, dominion, and majesty for ever'.

INTRODUCTION TO THE SECOND EPISTLE
OF PETER

The so-called Second Epistle of Peter envisages a situation similar to that of the Epistle of Jude, with certain additions. These are the arguments concerning the End of the world in chapter 3. The close resemblance to Jude and the reasons for believing that 2 Peter is secondary are discussed in the Introduction to Jude and 2 Peter above, pp. 65–69. The writer's object is to urge his readers to 'escape the corruption that is in the world because of passion, and become partakers of the divine nature' (cf. 1.4). This last expression sets him apart from all other writers of the New Testament, despite foreshadowings such as 'you have received the spirit of sonship' and we are 'heirs of God and fellow-heirs with Christ' (Rom. 8.15, 17), though the language echoes that of 1 Pet. 5.1, 'partakers in the glory that is to be revealed'; cf. Rom. 8.18, 'the glory that is to be revealed in us'. The writer does not quite imply, as the above (*RSV*) translation suggests, that participation in the divine nature consists in fleeing the world of sense; he says that the one who has been granted this gift by God will shun the world; he will make every effort to supplement faith with virtue, knowledge, self-control, steadfastness, godliness, brotherly affection, and love' (1.5ff.). Lack of these virtues prevents effective knowledge of Christ (1.8). This 'knowledge' takes the place of the Pauline 'faith' and is something different. Faith in this Epistle is either the Christian religion itself (1.1) or a virtue (1.5). In a similar manner, piety (godliness: 1.3, 6f.; 3.11) replaces holiness.

2 Pet. 2.1–3.3 consists of a paraphrase of the Epistle of Jude, using much of the original phraseology, though only once the same words (cf. 2 Pet. 2.17 with Jude 13 and see above, p. 67). Chapter 3 is largely concerned with the problem of the delay of a final judgment. The explanations given are (*a*) time is not the same for God as for man (3.8), and (*b*) the delay is due to God's forbearance. The curious thing about the treatment of this is that no unequivocal reference is made to the Second Coming of Christ beyond that in 1.16. It is not the coming of Christ but the 'coming of the Day of the Lord', the 'coming of the Day of God' which concerns the writer. 'The Day of God' (2 Pet. 3.12) is a particularly striking expression, partly

paralleled at Rev. 16.4. Jude also speaks of 'our God' (verse 4, cf. 2 Pet. 1.1; on this, see the commentary). The *parousia* imagery is not personal but cosmic: the disappearance of the heavens and the dissolution of the elements and the earth in fire: 'the day of the Lord will come like a thief, and then the heavens will pass away with a loud noise, and the elements will be dissolved with fire, and the earth and the works that are upon it will be burned up. Since all these things are thus to be dissolved, what sort of persons ought you to be in lives of holiness and godliness, waiting for and hastening the coming of the day of God, because of which the heavens will be kindled and dissolved, and the elements will melt with fire!' (3.10ff., 6f.). Nowhere in the New Testament and probably nowhere else in the Bible is the universe or the earth to be destroyed by fire (see on 3.7, 10). The nearest approach to all this in Jewish thought is in a passage from the Sibylline Oracles, deeply influenced by the ancient doctrine of the Great Year, according to which the earth was periodically renewed by fire (see on 3.10). 2 Peter also sees a new heaven and a new earth as a result (3.13). The writer's desire is not to inspire fear (even when he is following Jude he alters the sense of the warnings to that of hope for the righteous remnant: 2.4–10, especially verse 9) but to call to moral earnestness (3.14). The writer ends with a reference to 'our beloved brother Paul' as concurring in the necessity for godly behaviour, presumably because he was suspected of teaching that favoured laxity.

1. LITERARY AFFINITIES

2 Peter begins and ends in a manner reminiscent of 1 Peter: 2 Pet. 1.2=1 Pet. 1.1; 2 Pet. 3.16f. ('unstable', 'stability')=1 Pet. 5.12 ('stand fast'). The latter idea is also paralleled in Jude 24 ('keep you from falling'). Otherwise there is very little contact between the two works. 1 Peter is written in straightforward Hellenistic Greek, whereas 2 Peter affects a style that is almost literary, replete with quite uncommon words. The very first word in the Greek reads 'Symeon', a Hebraizing form of the name Simon that is only once used of Peter the Apostle in the relatively few places where it occurs at all in the New Testament, namely Ac. 15.14 (cf. Lk. 2.25, 34;

3.30; Ac. 13.1; Rev. 7.7). 1 Peter begins simply 'Peter'. It quotes the Old Testament, using the Septuagint version, whereas 2 Peter does not quote the Old Testament at all, but follows Jude in making up lists of warning illustrations from it. The nearest the writer gets to quotation is in 3.8 and 2.22 (cf. Ps. 90.4 and Prov. 26.11). Beyond this there may be a reference to Isa. 65.17; 66.22 in 3.13, though the idea of a new heaven and a new earth is widespread in Jewish sources (see the commentary *in loc.*); and Mic. 1.3f. has points of similarity with the theophany in 3.12, while the second half of 3.9 recalls Ezek. 33.11. The names used of Jesus and God are different in the two epistles, and in 2 Peter there is less Christology. The *parousia* is not the Second Coming of Christ so much as a divine theophany, the dissolution of the universe into the glory of God, represented in terms of fire; the passion and resurrection of Christ is not so much as once mentioned (cf. 1 Pet. 2.21ff.; 4.1; 1.3). Such contacts as do exist are mainly linguistic, and the ideas are different: cf. 1 Pet. 5.1 with 2 Pet. 1.4; 1 Pet. 3.20 with 2 Pet. 2.5.

The use of the Old Testament in 2 Peter has been noticed above, and the nearest approximation to be found there to the author's peculiar doctrine of universal conflagration. This is much closer to the teachings of the Sibylline Oracles and the Thanksgiving Psalms of the Dead Sea Sect: the matter is treated fully in the note on 3.10.

Alone in the New Testament outside the Gospels 2 Pet. 1.16ff. makes reference to the account of the Transfiguration. But direct linguistic dependence on the Synoptic record cannot be established: 3.10 is not a case in point, since there is closer correspondence to the 'thief' saying elsewhere in the New Testament (see the commentary there).

The writer knows of a collection of Pauline epistles (3.15f.), but shows very little influence from them in his work—much less than Jude. Here and there are points of contact, for instance 'the day of the Lord comes as a thief' in 1 Th. 5.2, cf. 2 Pet. 3.10, though this is a floating saying: see Rev. 16.4, which also refers in odd phrase to the 'day of God' (2 Pet. 3.12), and Mt. 24.43; Lk. 12.39. The Pastoral Epistles provide far more parallels. Here is, in fact, the *milieu* of this epistle. The word 'godliness' (piety) appears in 2 Peter at 1.3, 6, 7; 3.11; and in the Pastorals at 1 Tim. 2.2; 3.16; 4.7, 8; 6.3, 5, 6, 11;

2 Tim. 3.5; Tit. 1.1 and nowhere else in the New Testament except
in Ac. 3.12 where Peter disclaims that his or John's piety has made
the man walk at the Beautiful Gate of the Temple. The use of the
word 'faith' in 2 Peter of the Christian religion itself or a virtue is
paralleled in the Pastorals, where it occurs thirty-three times. 'Myths'
(of the kind spun by an incipient gnosticism) are referred to in
2 Pet. 1.16 and in 1 Tim. 1.4; 4.7; 2 Tim. 4.4; Tit. 1.14. 'Remind'
(a word typical of an age of 'looking back') appears at 1.12; 3.1;
and in 2 Tim. 2.14; Tit. 3.1 as well as Jude 5. The most obvious
relationship of 2 Peter is, of course, with Jude, and this has been dealt
with in detail above (pp. 65–69).

2. DATE

These affinities are clues to the date of the Epistle. The type of religion
envisaged is entirely different from that of the first age of Christians,
and different from that in 1 Peter. Holiness is replaced by piety, hope
by knowledge. The author points back to the events of the early
days: in 3.4 'the fathers' (now dead) are the first generation of
Christians; the Pauline epistles are now classed with 'the other
scriptures' (3.15f.); indeed the 'predictions of the holy prophets'
mentioned here and there (1.20; 3.2) may be those contained in the
New Testament scriptures. The expression 'partakers of the divine
nature' (1.4) sounds late. Irenaeus (c. 130–200) wrote: 'The word of
God, our Lord Jesus Christ, became what we are that he might
bring us to be what he is. . . .' Athanasius (298–373) wrote: 'He
became man that we might be made God.' This is the doctrine of
'deification', and it may be argued that it is too strong a term for
Irenaeus' position; but this only makes the expression in 2 Peter
sound later. The split in the writer's mind is also not between good
and evil but between the divine nature and the corruption of passion
and the defilements of the world (1.4; 2.20). This is a distinct advance
towards Hellenism and the day of gnosticism. The Epistle is certainly
later than that of Jude on which it is dependent; and the situation
assumed in it has also developed since Jude's time. The beliefs of the
heretics are more clearly defined; they profess to offer freedom (2.19);
they scoff at the doctrine of the End of the world (3.4); they have

'cleverly devised myths' (1.16), and are perhaps regarded as having more of a pseudo-philosophical backing. The quotations from the *Assumption of Moses* and 1 Enoch in Jude 9 and 14f. have been dropped; instead the examples have been generalized so as to obscure their origin in a day when presumably these pseudepigraphical works were going out of favour (2.4ff., 17). Finally the lateness of the epistle is indicated by the doxology addressed not to God the Father but to Christ (3.18). Still the position of the heretics seems undeveloped compared with that of the sects described by Irenaeus and we must assume that 2 Peter is earlier than their time. If Jude has been placed at before 120, 2 Peter may be placed somewhat later, say 130. This agrees with the fact that evidence of it is wanting in the Apostolic Fathers. A phrase in the Epistle of the Churches of Lyons and Vienne gives an idea of the sort of parallel that is suggested from the second century: 'not ineffective and unfruitful'; cf. 2 Pet. 1.8 (Eusebius, *H.E.* V.1.45).

3. AUTHORSHIP

Doubts about the authorship of 2 Peter go back to the earliest days; as with James, there was no unanimity about it by *c.* 200. Origen (*c.* 185–254) reports that its genuineness is 'disputed', though he himself accepts it. Eusebius, in the next century, recognized only one Epistle of Peter as genuine. In Jerome's time many distinguished between the author of 1 and 2 Peter on grounds of style. As we have seen, there are great differences. Whether or not, however, 1 Peter is by the Apostle, 2 Peter makes great efforts to be accepted as genuine, efforts which give the impression of being overdone. The author emphasizes the assumed authority of Peter (1.13–19). There is an elaborate attempt to give verisimilitude to the proceeding by a reference to the Transfiguration as if by an eyewitness (1.16ff.), to a prophecy of the Lord that he will soon die (1.13f.), to the first Epistle (3.1), and to Paul as a 'beloved brother' and fellow-Apostle (3.15). But the mention of 1 Peter in 2 Pet. 3.1ff. does not really fit that work (for it is too involved to posit another Petrine Epistle beside our 1 Peter). The future tense is used in 2.1ff. of the matters which will occupy the readers of the Epistle, namely the heresy attacked in it; but this gives way to the present in 2.10 and even the past in 2.15: in other words, the events supposed to be prophesied about by Peter have already begun to take place in the author's day. In fact, 1.15 expressly says that the Epistle is designed for a time after Peter's death, which seems contrived. Such a sentence as 3.1, 'that you should remember the predictions of the holy prophets and the commandment of the Lord and Saviour through your apostles' sounds odd in the mouth of Peter. But the case is decisive against Petrine authorship when the writer says, 'ever since the fathers [i.e. the first Christian generation] fell asleep' (3.4) and refers to a corpus of Pauline epistles already in existence and regarded as 'scripture' (3.15f.). 2 Peter must be considered pseudonymous, but it is vastly superior to the other numerous 'Petrine' works, the *Apocalypse of Peter*, the *Preaching of Peter*, the *Gospel of Peter*, the *Acts of Peter*, not to mention the fresh 'Acts' and 'Apocalypse' discovered at Nag Hammadi. Since the whole point of a pseudepigraph is to obscure the author's real identity there is no hope at all of establishing it. The custom of a disciple writing under the name of a famous teacher or leader was well established in the ancient world, and the prevalence of apocalypses such as we have had cause to mention more than once, going under the name of patriarchs like Moses and Enoch goes to show the popularity of such a fashion among the Jews. It is, however, too much to say that no one was ever deceived by the device, and the author of 2 Peter endeavours to see to it that the full force of his assumed personality is brought to bear. It has only to be remembered that the early Church was not unconcerned whether the letters were genuine or not, as is proved by the controversy over their admittance into the canon. Nevertheless, the fact remains that our conventions about copyright were not those of the first century.

4. DESTINATION

The heresy tackled in Jude appears to have been sufficiently general at least in a certain area for the writer of 2 Peter to be able simply to take it up into his own work with suitable emendations and additions, namely on the question of the End of the world, in order to bring it up to date and re-issue it for his own purposes. Its destination is wholly obscure, except that it is unlikely that 2.22 was included in a letter addressed to Jews, with its proverb from the widespread tale of Aḥikar. Even if the Jews were Christians they would be unlikely to take in their stride a familiar reference to the ways of carefully tended domestic swine. That the Epistle was not accepted in the Syriac-speaking Church is shown by its exclusion from the Peshitta version.

THE SECOND LETTER OF

PETER

THE SECOND LETTER OF

PETER

1 Simon Peter, a servant and apostle of Jesus Christ.
To those who have obtained a faith of equal standing with
ours in the righteousness of our God and Saviour Jesus Christ:

THE SALUTATION 1.1–2

The introduction seems to be based on the opening of 1 Peter, with significant
additions, e.g., the mention of 'knowledge'.

Simon: i.e., 'Symeon', a Hebraizing form of the name; it occurs elsewhere, in
Luke-Acts and Revelation (Lk. 2.25, 34; 3.30; Ac. 13.1; 15.14; Rev. 7.7). 1 Peter
uses 'Simon', the form popular among Greek-speaking Christians.

servant: i.e., slave. See on Jas 1.1.

apostle: the Greek translation of a Hebrew or Aramaic word for an agent. The
writer claims to be the apostle Peter.

who have obtained: i.e., whose *lot* has been to obtain, *sc.* through the grace of
God.

a faith: the word is certainly not used in the same sense as at verse 5, and it is
hard to see how 'faith' in the Pauline sense could be 'of equal standing' with any
other manifestation of it. No doubt, as in Jude 3, 20, it means 'the faith', belief in
Jesus Christ and what it entails. The Christianity of the second generation is
equally worth having with that of the first; cf. 1.15 where the letter is said to be
designed for those who come after Peter's death.

of equal standing: 'of the same kind.' See above.

in the righteousness of: perhaps 'by the righteousness of' in the sense that
'righteousness' in 2 Isaiah and Paul implies God's saving activity (cf. Isa. 46.13;
51.5; Rom. 1.16f.). But more probably the meaning is that the second generation
faith is as good as that of the first, by virtue of God's impartiality.

our God and Saviour Jesus Christ: a few MSS read 'Lord' for 'God'. It is possible
that the translation should be 'our God and the Saviour Jesus Christ' and so in
Tit. 2.13, 'the great God and our Saviour Jesus Christ' (but see the *RSV in loc.*).
It is difficult here in 2 Peter to see how the word 'righteousness' could be con-
strued with two persons; but see verse 3, where 'his' follows the same two. Moreover, God is called 'our Lord' at 3.15 and great stress is laid in that chapter on God
the Father's activity: cf. also Jude 4, 'persons who pervert the grace of our God . . .
and deny our only Master and Lord, Jesus Christ', and 25, 'to the only God,
our Saviour, through Jesus Christ our Lord'. Nevertheless, the New Testament

2 May grace and peace be multiplied to you in the knowledge of
God and of Jesus our Lord.

3 His divine power has granted to us all things that pertain to
life and godliness, through the knowledge of him who called us to

---

affords preparation for the mode of address to Jesus as God (cf. Heb. 1.8; Jn 20.28).
Ignatius (died c. 117) in his day had no hesitation in writing of Christ as God:
Epistle to the Ephesians 18.2, 'our God, Jesus the Christ, was conceived by Mary'.
Jesus is called 'Saviour' fourteen times in the New Testament, and the word is
used most frequently (of Christ or God) in the Pastoral Epistles and 2 Peter. It is
also important evidence that the doxology in 2 Pet. 3.18 is addressed to Christ,
which is unusual in the New Testament. The expression 'our Lord and Master
[the same word as in 2.1] Jesus Christ our God and Saviour' occurs in a Christian
formula of a much later date, and it is not impossible that this language was taken
over very early from the titles arrogated to themselves by pagan kings and
emperors.

2. May grace and peace be multiplied: cf. 1 Pet. 1.2 and see on Jude 2.

in the knowledge: Greek *epignōsis*. Not faith but knowledge is the theme of the
epistle. This word appears in it four times and another (*gnōsis*) three times (two of
them in the same verse). No distinction in meaning can be drawn between the
two words: cf. this verse with 3.18. 'Knowledge' in gnostic systems (e.g., Hermetism) could have a religious significance, but often implied the magical efficacy of
esoteric information about the structure of the universe, the creation of the world
and the nature of the true God. Instead of this 2 Peter speaks of 'the knowledge of
God and of Jesus our Lord'.

PARTICIPATION IN THE DIVINE NATURE AND ESCAPE
FROM CORRUPTION 1.3-11

THE GIFT AND CALLING OF GOD 1.3-4

3. His seems to refer to God, in contrast to 'him' and 'his' later in the verse.
His divine power is a reverential periphrasis for God. 'Power' is one of the
key-words of the epistle.
godliness: except for once in Acts (3.12) the word only occurs in the Pastorals
(ten times) and 2 Peter (four times). Piety has replaced the glorious liberty of the
children of God (Rom. 8.21). Liberty can lead to licence, and is already doing so
among those who profess it (cf. 2.2 and Jude 4). This must not be taken to imply,
however, as is often done, that sub-apostolic Christianity represented a serious
declension in spiritual power.
him who called us: i.e., Christ: cf. 1 Pet. 2.9.

his own glory and excellence, ⁴ by which he has granted to us his
precious and very great promises, that through these you may
escape from the corruption that is in the world because of passion,
and become partakers of the divine nature. ⁵ For this very reason
make every effort to supplement your faith with virtue, and virtue
with knowledge, ⁶ and knowledge with self-control, and self-
control with steadfastness, and steadfastness with godliness, ⁷ and
godliness with brotherly affection, and brotherly affection with love.
⁸ For if these things are yours and abound, they keep you from being
ineffective or unfruitful in the knowledge of our Lord Jesus Christ.

---

to his own glory: or, 'by his own glory'. The divinity of Christ is emphasized,
especially if the first reading is preferred (as in the *RSV*): it is 'his own' glory that
he calls men *to*.

excellence: i.e., 'virtue' in the Greek sense; e.g., the virtue of a runner is his speed,
of a knife its sharpness. Christ's virtue is his divine nature. Virtue and glory are
treated as synonymous in the LXX: Isa. 42.8, 12. In Hellenistic usage 'virtue' of
God=miracle, manifestation of divine power. The word implies morality in
verse 5, but although the epistle is largely concerned with its inculcation it is
unlikely that Christ's moral excellence is in question, for the writer makes little
of his example or person.

4. promises: the succeeding words describe the content of these.

that . . . you may escape: in the Greek these words occur after 'and become
partakers of the divine nature', suggesting that the partaking enables the escape
rather than that the escape is the means to 'deification' as in the contemporary
Hellenistic beliefs.

corruption that is in the world because of passion: Hellenistic religion saw
the main source of evil in matter, and therefore in bodily passions, and the main
need to be deliverance from the decay that is inseparable from life. This penetrated
deeply into Jewish thought, so that *The Testaments of the Twelve Patriarchs*, for
example, berates lust more than the Old Testament does, and Paul is remarkably
un-Hebrew in his championship of celibacy, whatever his eschatological expectations (cf. also Rev. 14.4). But the later books of the New Testament show still
more sensitivity in this direction.

become partakers of the divine nature: this is the strikingly original note in
2 Peter. Nowhere in the New Testament is there a parallel, though the gift of the
Spirit of God and of sonship is practically equivalent. Paul writes (Rom. 8.15ff.):
'You have received the spirit of sonship. When we cry, "Abba! Father!" it is the
Spirit himself bearing witness with our spirit that we are children of God, and if
children, then heirs, heirs of God and fellow heirs with Christ.' The language also

echoes 1 Pet. 5.1, 'partakers in the glory that is to be revealed'; cf. Rom. 8.18, 'the glory that is to be revealed in us'. But in 2 Peter the language is more metaphysical, patterned on that used in contemporary Hellenistic religion. The believer shares in a divine nature instead of a worldly. It is remarkable that it is the *individual* who is to attain to this, and not the Christian body as a whole.

HOW THIS IS TO BE ACHIEVED 1.5-11

5. For this very reason: the 'deification' is closely connected with moral virtues.

faith: faith is taken here on all fours with moral virtues.

virtue: cf. Phil. 4.8. The meaning is the quite general one of moral excellence, and not of any particular virtue.

knowledge: the word *gnōsis* is here used of moral virtue (i.e., close to wisdom) (cf. 2 C. 6.6). In the *Corpus Hermeticum* 1 (i.e., *Poimandres*). 27 the seer (identified before the final formation of the Corpus with Hermes), after having been empowered and instructed in the nature of the All and the supreme vision, begins to preach 'the beauty of godliness and knowledge'. He cries, 'O peoples, men born of earth, who have given yourselves over to drunkenness, to sleep and ignorance of God, be sober', etc. Cf. *The Gospel of Thomas* log. 28, 'Jesus said, I stood in the midst of the world and in flesh I appeared to them; I found them all drunk, and none among them athirst'.

6. self-control: i.e., continence; cf. e.g., 1 Clem. 35.2.

steadfastness: i.e., endurance, perseverance, fortitude—an oft-mentioned virtue in the New Testament.

7. brotherly affection: lit., love of blood brothers and sisters; in a transferred sense of Christians for each other.

love: *Agapē*, the characteristic Christian virtue (cf. 1 C. 13), is that to which all the list has been leading. First of all that in God which impels him towards man it is the factor which draws men together in mutual caring, and sends them also to those outside. With this list of virtues cf. that in Hermas: *Vis.* 3.8.3ff., which consists of faith, self-control (i.e. continence), simplicity, understanding innocence, reverence, and love; virtues which are represented as daughters of (i.e., derived from) each other, as possibly here. The list was apparently a catechetical one.

8. abound: or, increase. The way to heaven (verse 11) is the practice of the Christian life.

ineffective or unfruitful: in the second-century Epistle of the Churches of Lyons and Vienne, the time spent by the martyrs awaiting death is described as 'not ineffective or unfruitful'. Cf. the Odes of Solomon 11.23,

'For there is abundant room in thy Paradise;
And nothing is useless therein:
But everything is filled with fruit' (Harris-Mingana translation).

⁹ For whoever lacks these things is blind and shortsighted and has forgotten that he was cleansed from his old sins. ¹⁰ Therefore, brethren, be the more zealous to confirm your call and election, for if you do this you will never fall; ¹¹ so there will be richly provided for you an entrance into the eternal kingdom of our Lord and Saviour Jesus Christ.

12 Therefore I intend always to remind you of these things, though you know them and are established in the truth that you have. ¹³ I think it right, as long as I am in this body, to arouse you by way of reminder, ¹⁴ since I know that the putting off of my body

---

9. cleansed from his old sins: i.e., in baptism.

10. confirm your call: God calls, but his call is not the *fiat* of crushing omnipotence: man confirms his own calling. Cf. Phil. 2.12f. for the classic statement of the relation between grace and the faith that includes works: 'Work out your own salvation with fear and trembling, for God is at work in you, both to will and work for his good pleasure.' See also on Jas 2.18.

election: lit., 'choice'. Cf. Jn 15.16, 'You did not choose me, but I chose you and appointed you that you should go and bear fruit and that your fruit should abide; so that whatever you ask the Father in my name, he may give you.' Christ calls and chooses the faithful; they are not self-appointed. This call and choice is to an eternal inheritance, a relationship with the ultimate, the source and sustainer of all good. Cf. on Jas 2.5.

never fall: i.e., never seriously err.

11. provided for you: God is the initiator and his grace primary.

entrance: cf. Heb. 10.19.

kingdom: see on Jas 2.5. In Jesus' teaching the kingdom is God's except in late strata of the Synoptic tradition, e.g., Mt. 13.41 (cf. Rev. 11.15).

PURPOSE OF THE EPISTLE TO RECALL TO THE FAITH
1.12–21

THE AUTHOR SPEAKS DIRECTLY IN THE PERSON OF PETER 1.12–15

12. Cf. Jude 5 for the source of the language of this verse.

truth: *sc.* of the Christian faith.

13. body: lit., tent; cf. 2 C. 5.1. In Jn 1.14 'dwelt' is literally 'tabernacled', using the same metaphor of the tent. The three 'booths' mentioned by Peter at the Transfiguration (Mk 9.5) may be in mind: cf. verse 17 below.

arouse: cf. Rom. 13.11.

14. putting off of my body (lit., 'tent'). Curious mixture of metaphors. In 1 Pet. 3.21 the word is used for removing dirt from the body.

will be soon, as our Lord Jesus Christ showed me. ¹⁵And I will see
to it that after my departure you may be able at any time to recall
these things.

16 For we did not follow cleverly devised myths when we made
known to you the power and coming of our Lord Jesus Christ, but
we were eyewitnesses of his majesty. ¹⁷ For when he received honour

---

as our Lord Jesus Christ showed me: this may refer to Jn 21.18f. but since the
imminence of death seems at issue probably some other occasion is in mind,
perhaps from an early form of the *Quo vadis* story.

15. The reference may be to the Gospel of Mark, which tradition associates
with Peter, but this had been in circulation long before this epistle was published.
The epistle itself may be in question, but the future tense makes this difficult.
Considerable apocryphal literature was composed in the name of Peter.

departure: lit., 'exodus', as in Lk. 9.31, also in connection with the Transfiguration.

THE FACTUAL BASIS OF THE APOSTOLIC TESTIMONY 1.16-21

The facts are those of the Transfiguration, as recorded in the Synoptics. No
other New Testament writer uses the tradition in this way.

16. we: that is, the Apostles.

cleverly devised myths: such as those expounded by the gnostics, to whom
history was abhorrent, and speculation the essence of truth (cf. 1 Tim. 1.4; 4.7;
2 Tim. 4.4; Tit. 1.14).

coming: in Greek *parousia*, the technical term for the Second Coming of Christ.
The word was used of a state visit and often connected with 'power'; but cf.
verse 3 above and Mt. 24.30; Mk 9.1. It also referred to a divine theophany in
pagan circles, and the present author appears to think of it in terms of the Old
Testament theophanies: see 3.12f. and verses 19ff. below. It could be used of any
coming, e.g., that of Titus (2 C. 7.6), or Antichrist (2 Th. 2.9). 2 Peter uses it of
the Second Coming or final judgment in 3.4 and of the 'day of God' in 3.12.
Here, however, no distinction is drawn between the First and Second Comings.
The power and majesty of Christ were shown in the Transfiguration (the word
parousia is used of the First Coming in Justin Martyr: 1 *Apol.* 48, referring to
Isa. 35.4ff., 'At his coming the lame shall leap as a hart', etc.). The glory shown for a
moment then is the same that will be revealed (cf. 1 Pet. 1.5, and on Jas 5.7).

eyewitnesses: the Greek word signifies those who have been initiated into the
pagan 'mysteries' and seen the theophanies.

majesty: cf. Lk. 9.43 (of the wonder of God shown in a healing); Ac. 19.27 (of
Artemis).

17. honour and glory. The two words belong together (cf. Ps. 8.4f.) and are

and glory from God the Father and the voice was borne to him by the Majestic Glory, 'This is my beloved Son, with whom I am well pleased,' [18] we heard this voice borne from heaven, for we were with him on the holy mountain. [19]And we have the prophetic word

---

used together in the Johannine gospel, where the word is said to have 'tabernacled' with men (cf. Jn 1.14 and above on verse 13).

the voice was borne to him by the majestic Glory: the majestic Glory is God in the Shekinah or cloud of the divine glory; the voice is the *bath ḳōl*. Both are Jewish imagery for the presence of God, but their use was fully taken over by Gentile Christianity. The voice came out of the cloud (Mk 9.7). The Transfiguration is thought of as in the Synoptics as confirming belief in Christ's person, though not (as there) his teaching office. So it is chosen to confirm the teaching mission of the apostles as against the work of false teachers. The notion of divine theophanies like those in the Old Testament (e.g., Sinai) is probably also in the writer's mind. The language is different from that in the rest of the New Testament and, 'the Majestic Glory' recalls the apocryphal writings.

borne . . . by the Majestic Glory is a curious expression. Some versions (Vulgate and inferior Syriac) have 'from', an obvious correction: cf. verse 18. In *Poimandres* (*CH* 1.5) the 'spiritual Word' is 'borne' over or upon the primeval chaos: cf. Gen. 1.2, LXX.

This is my beloved Son . . . : cf. Mk 9.7 and parallels with Mt. 3.17 and parallels. Also Ps. 2.7. 'Beloved Son' is practically equivalent to 'only Son' (cf. Gen. 22.2, LXX, etc.).

with whom I am well pleased: equivalent to 'my chosen', 'the one on whom my purpose rests' (cf. Isa. 42:1).

18. Reiteration that the Apostles were eyewitnesses, and that the writer was one of them.

the holy mountain of Transfiguration.

19. the prophetic word: perhaps the Old Testament prophecies foreshadowing the Second Coming, though, if so, further mention is held over until 3.2; but to take an incident of Christ's ministry as confirming Old Testament prophecies is a curious reversal of New Testament procedure, whereby these confirm the Gospel events. It would be more natural to take the references to 'holy prophets' in 3.2 and here as meaning New Testament prophets (cf. Eph. 2.20; 3.5; 4.11; where this is apparently the case) and 'scriptures' in verse 20 as referring to the New Testament itself (cf. 3.16). The author offers no proof texts as would be called for on either view. But the New Testament abounds in prophecies of cynicism and licence and false teaching in the last time: Mk 13.22; 2 Th. 2.9; 1 Jn 2.18f.; Jude 4; contrast Mal. 4.5f. When he does return to the question of these 'predictions of the holy prophets' at 3.2, the author is, in fact, echoing words of Jude that would

made more sure. You will do well to pay attention to this as to a lamp shining in a dark place, until the day dawns and the morning star rises in your hearts. [20] First of all you must understand this, that no prophecy of scripture is a matter of one's own interpretation, [21] because no prophecy ever came by the impulse of man, but men moved by the Holy Spirit spoke from God.

---

seem to confirm this view: 'You must remember, beloved, the predictions of the apostles of our Lord Jesus Christ; they said to you, "In the last time there will be scoffers, following their own ungodly passions".' The Transfiguration comes in as a glimpse of the power and glory of Jesus to the memory of which the faithful must cling 'until the day dawns' with its full light. But in 2.1 the Old Testament prophets are certainly meant; the author therefore does not discriminate between the two sorts.

You will do well: the normal way of saying 'please' in the papyri: cf. Jas 2.3, where the same expression occurs.

a lamp shining in a dark place: cf. Mk 4.21; Jn 5.35 (see Sir. 48.1); 1.5. The image is used of Elijah, John the Baptist, and the word of Christ; here it is the message of the apostles who saw the glory before its due time that is intended.

the day: cf. 3.12. The coming of the glory of God throughout the whole universe by its complete transformation, when all will become clear (cf. Rom. 13.12).

the morning star: Venus, herald of dawn: cf. the similar idea in Lk. 1.78. There, however, not a star but day itself is intended, and it has been suggested that the sun is meant here.

rises in your hearts: the writer is aware of a spiritual significance in the doctrine of the Second Coming. It is no mere external manifestation of supreme might, however bizarre his imagery may be (cf. 3.10). The illumination of the day is illumination of the minds and spirits of the believers. 'The day dawns' is parallel to 'the morning star rises in your hearts', and the form of the latter sentence is not without interest. Commentators have sometimes sought to alter the implications of 'in your hearts' in this context by taking it as the beginning of the next verse

20. no prophecy . . . is a matter of one's own interpretation: presumably. the meaning is that private interpretation must give way to the authoritative interpretations of the Church, inspired by the Spirit.

21. Prophecy came in the first place under the inspiration of God; therefore the Holy Spirit must interpret it: see on the next verse.

no prophecy ever came: lit., 'was borne' , cf. verse 17.

men moved by the Holy Spirit: lit., 'borne' by the Holy Spirit. In the Old Testament the prophet is 'the man of the Spirit' (the parallelism identifies the two in Hos. 9.7), i.e., the man possessed by the Spirit and not in any way the manipulator of divine powers. Cf. Ac. 8.39 (where the Spirit catches up Philip) with

2 But false prophets also arose among the people, just as there will be false teachers among you, who will secretly bring in destructive heresies, even denying the Master who bought them, bringing

---

I Kg. 18.46 (Elijah runs before Ahab: the Spirit is not specifically mentioned, but for 'hand of the Lord'='Spirit' see Lk. 11.20 and Mt. 12.28. The Spirit gives superhuman power (Jg. 14.6; I Sam. 11.6f.), sets prophets in a frenzy (I Sam. 10.10; 19.20ff.), is responsible for intellectual and artistic achievement (Exod. 35.30–36.1), and 'speaks by the prophets': see especially Isa. 61.1ff. In the New Testament the anointing with the Spirit is what constitutes Jesus the 'Christ', i.e., anointed. In Lk. 4.18 the Isaiah passage is quoted, as defining the works for which he is anointed by the Spirit; Ac. 10.38 recalls 'how God anointed Jesus of Nazareth with the Holy Spirit and with power, and he went about doing good and healing all who were oppressed by the devil, for God was with him'. The Spirit gives gifts of wisdom, faith, healing, tongues and prophecy (I C. 12.8ff.; 14.2f.), the fruits of the Spirit are moral and religious qualities (Gal. 5.22). All these abilities and powers are gifts from God, exercised by his inspiration, for the Spirit is a personal being. Therefore **no prophecy ever came by the impulse of man**; interpretation is not an arbitrary matter of individual whim.

THE FALSE TEACHERS 2.1–22

Throughout this chapter the author draws heavily upon the thought of the Epistle of Jude, paraphrasing the language.

1. false prophets also arose: cf. Dt. 13.2ff.; Jer. 14.14; 23.14; Mt. 24.11, 24. The *Didache* gives rules for detecting false prophets among Christians.

the people: i.e., Israel.

there will be: the author speaks in the future tense because he is supposed to be Peter speaking of conditions after his death; but cf. 10 and 20f., where the use of the present and past tenses shows that the events described are already occurring.

false teachers: cf. Mt. 7.15; Ac. 20.29; I Tim. 4.1, etc., and Jude 4. Many references to preachers of falsehood occur in the Hymns of the Dead Sea Sect.

heresies: the word originally meant schools of thought or sects and differing opinions, then schisms in the Church (I C. 11.18f.), and finally false doctrines (Ignatius: *Eph.* 6.2; *Trall.* 6.1). It is contrasted with 'way' in Ac. 24.14, cf. the next verse of 2 Peter.

denying: cf. Jude 4 and the note there. No reference exists here to Peter's 'denial' as recorded in the Synoptics; the heretics rejected what Christ stood for in a more radical way.

Master: the word used means the lord of a slave, and it is never used of Jesus (as apparently here and at Jude 4) elsewhere in the New Testament. It is used of God five times (Lk. 2.29; Ac. 4.24; 2 Tim. 2.21), and of slave-owners four times (I Tim. 6.1f. (*bis*); Tit. 2.9; I Pet. 2.18).

upon themselves swift destruction. ² And many will follow their
licentiousness, and because of them the way of truth will be reviled.
³And in their greed they will exploit you with false words; from of
old their condemnation has not been idle, and their destruction has
not been asleep.

4 For if God did not spare the angels when they sinned, but cast
them into hell and committed them to pits of nether gloom to be
kept until the judgment; ⁵ if he did not spare the ancient world, but

---

bought: the image is of the purchase of a slave (cf. 1. C. 6.20).
swift: imminent. Cf. 3.10 which, however, rests uneasily alongside 3.9, with its
message that the final reckoning could be indefiitely postponed (cf. also 3.15).
destruction: the Akhmim Fragment of the *Apocalypse of Peter* begins with a
prophecy of Jesus: 'Many of them shall be false prophets, and shall teach ways of
destruction.'
  2. The heretics practised immorality (cˠ Jude 4).
way of truth: a Hebraism meaning 'the true way'. 'The Way' was the earliest
name for the Church, as befits a community sprung from Judaism, which lays all
emphasis upon practice: cf. Ac. 9.2 and *passim*; also Jn 14.4ff. and especially 6.
2 Peter uses the expression in a manner which rather suggests the later *ho kanōn tēs
alētheias, regula veritatis*. In Gen. 24.48 'the way of truth' means 'the right way'.
See also Ps. 118 (119).31 LXX and Jude 11; 2 Pet. 2.15 (*bis*), 21; also Jn 14.4ff.
  3. they will exploit you: see on Jude 11, 16.
from of old their condemnation: see Jude 4 and the note there.
  4ff. The author uses two examples of judgment from Jude (the angels and
Sodomites) and adds the Flood, possibly under the influence of 1 Pet. 3.20. Perhaps
under the same influence he stresses the power of God to rescue the oppressed
individual or righteous remnant rather than the theme of punishment which
informs the parallel passage in Jude.
  4. the angels: see on Jude 6 and the Introduction, p. 68. The language of
2 Peter is not so close to Hesiod as that of Jude except that the writer uses a verb
from the same word 'Tartarus', translated here **hell**. The word also occurs in
1 Enoch 20.2. So does **'pits'**; but 2 Peter significantly omits all reference to the
apocryphal writing. Some MSS have a similar word (*sirais* for *sirois*) meaning
'chains': cf. the parallel in Jude, 'kept by him in eternal chains in the nether gloom'.
The judgment of the angels is a widespread theme, and crops up in the Dead Sea
Scrolls: 1QH 10.34.
  5. herald: 'preacher', cf. 1 Tim. 2.7 and 1 Clem. 7.6, 'Noah preached repentance
and those who obeyed were saved'. There was a widespread Jewish tradition that
Noah preached to the generation of the Flood. The account of Josephus
(*Antiquities* I.3.1) uses language similar to that about Lot in verse 7: 'Many angels

preserved Noah, a herald of righteousness, with seven other persons, when he brought a flood upon the world of the ungodly; **⁶** if by turning the cities of Sodom and Gomor′rah to ashes he condemned them to extinction and made them an example to those who were to be ungodly; **⁷** and if he rescued righteous Lot, greatly distressed by the licentiousness of the wicked **⁸** (for by what that righteous man saw and heard as he lived among them, he was vexed in his righteous soul day after day with their lawless deeds), **⁹** then the Lord knows how to rescue the godly from trial, and to keep the unrighteous under punishment until the day of judgment, **¹⁰** and especially those who indulge in the lust of defiling passion and despise authority.

---

of God lay with women and begot sons that proved violent, and despisers of all goodness, on account of the confidence they had in their own strength, for the tradition is that they did the same things as they whom the Greeks call giants. But Noah was very uneasy at what they did, and being displeased with their behaviour tried to persuade them to change their dispositions and deeds for the better.'

with seven other persons: cf. 1 Pet. 3.20. Lit., the eighth (man), which some have taken to mean the eighth from Adam. According to Gen. 4 and 5.28f., Noah was, in fact, the eighth from Adam. But according to Gen. 5, Enoch was the seventh from Adam (the tradition followed by 1 Enoch and Jude 14) and Noah the tenth.

6. *The men of Sodom and the rescue of Lot*: cf. Jude 7; 3 Mac. 2.4f.

turning . . . to ashes: lit., 'covering with ashes', as in a volcanic eruption.

7. Cf. Wis. 10.6, 'While the ungodly were perishing, Wisdom rescued a righteous man, when he fled from the fire that descended out of heaven on the five cities'; also 1 Clem. 11.1, 'For his hospitality and piety Lot was saved out of Sodom when the whole countryside was judged by fire and brimstone, and the Master made it clear that he does not forsake those who hope in him, but gives over to punishme. and torture those who turn to others': cf. verses 9f. (and verse 1 of this chapter, where the same word for 'Master' is used). The writer of 2 Peter turns here from the note of warning to that of encouragement.

8. what that righteous man saw was the 'trial' (verse 9) from which God delivered him.

9. The Lord knows how to rescue: i.e., the Lord can rescue. It is often assumed that the reference is specifically to the final Judgment (3.9f.), thought of as parallel to the catastrophe that overwhelmed Sodom and Gomorrah. But this cannot be if the ungodly at the time of this deliverance are to be kept **under punishment until the day of judgment.** It is to be noted that some doctrine of interim punishment is implied (as in the parable of the rich man and Lazarus).

Bold and wilful, they are not afraid to revile the glorious ones, ¹¹ whereas angels, though greater in might and power, do not pronounce a reviling judgment upon them before the Lord. ¹² But these, like irrational animals, creatures of instinct, born to be caught and killed, reviling in matters of which they are ignorant, will be destroyed in the same destruction with them, ¹³ suffering wrong for their wrongdoing. They count it pleasure to revel in the daytime. They are blots and blemishes, revelling in their dissipation, carousing with you. ¹⁴ They have eyes full of adultery, insatiable for sin. They entice unsteady souls. They have hearts trained in greed.

---

10. The heretics are licentious and despise authority. The warning is directed specifically against the people the author has in mind throughout the epistle. See on Jude 8.

11. See on Jude 9. 2 Peter generalizes and omits the example from the apocryphal *Assumption of Moses*.

them: i.e., the 'glorious ones' or 'glories', an order of angels. Jude says that Michael did not 'pronounce a reviling judgment' upon the devil.

12. See on Jude 10. The language is rearranged until the verse becomes virtually unintelligible: irrational animals do not 'revile in matters of which they are ignorant'. The difficulty is somewhat eased by placing a full stop after 'killed', and beginning a new sentence with 'Reviling'.

them: i.e., the irrational animals. The heretics are fit for extermination like vermin.

13. suffering wrong for their wrongdoing reproduces a play on words in the original. Another translation is, 'being deprived of the reward of their wrongdoing'. A variant reading gives yet a third: 'receiving the reward of their wrongdoing.'

to revel in the daytime: if this is a reference to the *Assumption of Moses* 7.4, 'lovers of banquets at every hour of the day', it is incongruous with the writer's unwillingness to associate himself with the pseudepigraphical literature, if that is the reason for his alterations of Jude. Perhaps the heretics did, in fact, 'revel in the daytime'.

dissipation: the word originally meant 'guile' and then 'pleasures': cf. Mk 4.19, where the word rendered 'cares' should probably read 'pleasures'. There is an alternative reading 'love-feasts' here as in the parallel Jude 12. The words are not altogether dissimilar: *agapais* and *apatais*.

14. eyes full of adultery: the original says 'eyes full of an adulteress' (cf. Mt. 5.28).

Accursed children! ¹⁵ Forsaking the right way they have gone astray; they have followed the way of Balaam, the son of Be or, who loved gain from wrongdoing, ¹⁶ but was rebuked for his own transgression; a dumb ass spoke with human voice and restrained the prophet's madness.

17 These are waterless springs and mists driven by a storm; for them the nether gloom of darkness has been reserved. ¹⁸ For, uttering loud boasts of folly, they entice with licentious passions of the flesh men who have barely escaped from those who live in error. ¹⁹ They promise them freedom, but they themselves are slaves of

---

Accursed children: lit., 'children of a curse': cf. 1 Pet. 1.14 which is translated by the *RSV* as a genitive of quality, 'disobedient children'; but the meaning is 'disobedient ones'. Cf. Eph. 2.2 'sons of disobedience'; 2.3 'children of wrath'; 5.8 'children of light'. This is a Semitic idiom derived by the author from the background of Christianity: see such phrases as 'sons of the East' (Gen. 29.1); 'son of man'; 'son of freedom' for free man; and Gen. 15.3; 1 Sam. 20.31; Jg. 19.22; Ezr. 4.1; Lam. 3.13, etc. We should therefore read, 'Accursed ones'. There is no reference to children at all.

THE EXAMPLE OF BALAAM 2.15–16

the right way: lit., 'straight way'. The same expression occurs in a Christian papyrus letter of the early fourth century found at Oxyrhynchus. The ways of the wicked are crooked: Prov. 2.15; cf. Mt. 24.4; 1 Jn 3.7 for the sort of misleading teaching envisaged. The Two Ways of life and death appear in the *Didache* (in 6.1 the way of life is called 'this way of the teaching') and in the last chapters of *Barnabas* (18ff.); the ways of good and evil, light and darkness appear in a long passage of the so-called 'Manual of Discipline' of the DSS. Cf. also Mt. 7.13f.= Lk. 13.23f. The notion was a commonplace of Jewish thought.
Balaam . . . who loved gain for wrongdoing. Cf. on Jude 11.
   16. Cf. Num. 22.28.

FURTHER DESCRIPTIONS AND DENUNCIATIONS 2.17–22

   17. See Jude 12f. The metaphors are mixed: 'the nether gloom of darkness' has not been reserved for 'waterless springs and mists'.
waterless springs: these are the false teachers, promising what they do not give (cf. verse 19). In Jude they are waterless clouds.
   18. See Jude 16.
men who have barely escaped: the Gentiles who lately lived as 'heathen . . . led astray by dumb idols' (1 C. 12.2). It is unlikely that the heretics them-

corruption; for whatever overcomes a man, to that he is enslaved.
20 For if, after they have escaped the defilements of the world
through the knowledge of our Lord and Saviour Jesus Christ, they
are again entangled in them and overpowered, the last state has
become worse for them than the first. **21** For it would have been
better for them never to have known the way of righteousness than
after knowing it to turn back from the holy commandment delivered
to them. **22** It has happened to them according to the true proverb,
The dog turns back to his own vomit, and the sow is washed only to
wallow in the mire.

---

selves are intended, for this would make the accusative refer to the subject of the
sentence.
   19. Cf. verses 17 and 1.3f. Those who prate of freedom are themselves slaves:
cf. Jn 8.34, 'whoever commits sin is the slave of sin'. See also Gal. 5.13.
   20. Either the false teachers themselves or the Gentiles mentioned in verse 18
are intended. It is almost certain to be the latter. The servitude of the teachers is
mentioned in verse 19 with them in mind. A comparison with the Johannine
teaching is instructive. John holds that eternal life is to 'know' God in Christ
(17.3) and that 'the world' is bereft of this acquaintance (17.25). 2 Peter is closer to
this than the gnostics, but closer to them than to John in his references to defilement and 'knowledge' (for the latter see 1.3; the noun never occurs in the Johannine
writings).
the last state has become worse than the first: cf. Mt. 12.45.
   21. Jesus said of Judas, 'It would have been better for that man if he had not
been born' (Mk 14.21). Cf. the dire warnings in Hebrews to those who turn back:
Heb. 10.26, 28f.; 12.25; 6.6.
holy commandment is equivalent to Jude's 'holy faith'. It is the moral side of
Christianity that is at stake.
   22. The dog turns back to his own vomit here means that the Gentiles have
reverted to type. The proverb occurs at Prov. 26.11 and elsewhere in Jewish
literature. Sometimes it is used loosely, as when a pupil returns to his own master
(*Yoma* 53b).
The sow is washed only to wallow in the mire: this proverb occurs in *The
Story of Ahikar*, a very popular tale in the ancient world, at 8.18 (Syriac; Arabic
15, Armenian 24). Swine naturally did not figure in Jewish proverbs. *Ahikar*
was probably originally an Assyrian tale; the Greeks knew of it; for example,
Democritus quotes this proverb (Clem. Alex: *Protrept.* 75). 2 Peter has already
likened the heretics themselves to 'irrational animals, caught to be killed' (verse
12).

3 This is now the second letter that I have written to you, beloved, and in both of them I have aroused your sincere mind by way of reminder; [2] that you should remember the predictions of the holy prophets and the commandment of the Lord and Saviour through your apostles. [3] First of all you must understand this, that scoffers will come in the last days with scoffing, following their own passions [4] and saying, 'Where is the promise of his coming? For

---

BELIEF IN THE END OF THE WORLD 3.1–13

The author turns to the subject of the delay in the expected coming of the 'day of the Lord'. He still shows some traces of Jude's language.

1. the second letter: this probably alludes to our 1 Peter, now well known in the Church.

sincere mind: Plato uses the expression of the 'pure reason' and the adjective of the soul that is fascinated by the body, its desires and pleasures (*Phaedo* 66A and 81C).

by way of reminder: cf. 1.13; Jude 5.

2. Cf. Jude 17.

holy prophets. See 1.19; 2.2 and the notes there. In Eph. 3.5 'holy apostles and prophets' are all evidently New Testament men. So it may well be here, especially in view of the fact that no Old Testament proof-texts follow.

your is used of the apostles to distinguish them from the false teachers and not from the prophets.

The sentence is difficult in the original, though the general meaning is clear enough.

commandment. The direction to the whole Christian life.

apostles: i.e., the Twelve.

3. Cf. Jude 18.

scoffers: the problem set by the delayed End apparently did not affect the faithful as a whole but only certain sceptical elements. Throughout its history Christianity has been notably independent of particular eschatological expectations.

the last days: equivalent to 'the last time' in Jude. For the actual phrase, cf. Heb. 1.2; also Jas 5.3; 1 Pet. 1.20.

4. 1. Clem. 23.3 reads, 'Let this scripture be far from us which says, "Miserable are the double-minded, who doubt in their soul and say, 'We have heard these things also in the days of our fathers, and behold, we have grown old and none of these has happened to us'"'. 2 Clem. 11.2 calls it 'a prophetic word'. Some have thought that it is a quotation from the Book of *Eldad and Modad*, cf. Hermas: *Vis.* 2.3.4, 'But you shall say to Maximus, "Behold, tribulation is coming, if you think fit to deny again". "The Lord is near to those who turn to

ever since the fathers fell asleep, all things have continued as they
were from the beginning of creation.' ⁵ They deliberately ignore
this fact, that by the word of God heavens existed long ago, and an

---

him", as it is written in *Eldad and Modad*, who prophesied to the people in the
wilderness'. For Eldad and Modad, see Num. 11.26 and on Jas 1.8; 4.5; 5.7).

the promise: i.e., the fulfilment of that promise.

coming: the technical term *parousia* for the Second Coming of Christ. See on
1.16.

the fathers: in the Book of Eldad and Modad 'our fathers' are presumably the
men of the wilderness generation; for 2 Peter and his readers the 'fathers' are the
previous generation of Christian believers.

fell asleep: i.e., died; cf. Jn 11.11; Ac. 7.60; 13.36; 1 C. 7.39; 11.30; 15.6, 18, 20,
51; 1 Th. 4.13ff. Paul's correspondents had been disturbed by the fact that their
friends had died before the *parousia*, and wondered if this meant that they had lost
their part in the resurrection (1 Th. 4.13–18, cf. 1 Pet. 4.6).

all things have continued as they were from the beginning of creation:.
i.e., the stability of the created order precludes the notion of a catastrophic end.
The author answers in the next verse that creation is not stable but was destroyed
once before and will be destroyed again. This contradicts the Noachic covenant
of Gen. 9.11, and the words of God in Gen. 8.21, 'I will never again curse the
ground . . . neither will I ever again destroy every living creature as I have done',
but 2 Peter could have quoted the next verse, '*While the earth remains*, seedtime
and harvest, cold and heat, summer and winter, day and night, shall not cease'.
The rabbis discussed the possibility that the Noachic covenant only obviated the
danger of destruction by water.

The philosophical doctrine of the eternity of creation seems to have appealed
to Philo, though it was firmly rejected by the rabbis. (*Gen. Rab.* 1.9 gives an
account of the contention between a philosopher and R. Gamaliel, who quoted
Isa. 45.7; Ps. 148.4f.; Am. 4.13; Prov. 8.24.)

5–7. 2 Peter is following a widespread theory according to which the earlier
destruction of the world by a Flood would be paralleled by another by fire.
This appears in *The Life of Adam and Eve* 49.3, 'Our Lord will bring upon your race
the anger of his judgment, first by water, the second time by fire; by these two
will the Lord judge the whole human race' (Wells' trans. in Charles). This is
followed by Eve's instructions to write accounts of Adam's life on stone and clay,
which would withstand water and fire respectively. (Josephus, who also carries
the tale: *Ant.* I.2.3, relates that *Adam* gave instructions for pillars of brick and stone
and that they still existed in his day). The notion also appears in the Talmud:
Zeb. 116a. It goes back to the Babylonian doctrine of the Great Year, according
o which a flood or a conflagration takes place periodically over vast stretches of

earth formed out of water and by means of water, 6 through which the world that then existed was deluged with water and perished. 7 But by the same word the heavens and earth that now exist have been stored up for fire, being kept until the day of judgment and destruction of ungodly men.

---

time when the planets are in a certain order. This doctrine became known in the West through a Babylonian priest called Berosus, who is mentioned by Josephus and referred to in this connection by the Stoic Seneca (*Quaest. nat.* 3.29).

5f. Here the whole world (*kosmos*) was destroyed by the Flood, in contrast to the biblical account, according to which only its inhabitants perished.

by the word of God: cf. the 'words' of God in Gen. 1 and Ps. 33.6ff., except that in those places they are creative, not destructive. This belief that God will destroy his creation is impossible to trace in the teaching of our Lord anywhere in the Gospels.

heavens existed . . . and an earth: both were created by the word of God and constituted the universe.

formed out of water and by means of water: cf. Gen. 1.2, 6ff.; Pss. 24.2; 136.6. The language is, however, more reminiscent of Thales' doctrine that water was the 'nature' of all that is.

6. through which is plural in the original, perhaps referring to the waters above the heavens and under the earth: Ps. 148.4; Exod. 20.4.

the world . . . perished: the word *kosmos* need not necessarily mean the universe, the sum total of all that is, but the author apparently takes the account of the Flood to imply a complete destruction of the created world by water. In 1 Enoch 83 Enoch tells his son Methuselah of a vision of the future in which the heaven collapses on to the earth, which is then swallowed up in an abyss; this may refer to the Flood.

7. fire: see above. The notion that the earth was periodically destroyed by fire was Babylonian, but also occurred in the Stoic doctrine that the world was renewed by being converted into fire. The Persians thought of the purification of men at the final Rehabilitation as effected by molten metal. The notion of the destruction of the world by fire occurs nowhere else in the New Testament or the Old Testament either. Fire is involved in judgment and wrath: cf. Isa. 66.15f.; Ezek. 36.5; Zeph. 1.18; 3.8; 1 C. 3.13; Ps. 97.3; Dan. 7.9f; Mt. 3.10, 12 (John the Baptist; cf. verse 11, where fire is associated with the Holy Spirit: in Zoroastrianism they are identified). Hell contains or consists of fire in Jewish belief which is reflected in such passages as Mt. 25.41; Mk 9.43; Lk. 16.24; Rev. 20.14; 21.8.

being kept until the day of judgment, etc: see on Jude 6. The word 'kept' is popular with both writers: 2 Pet. 2.4, 9, 17; 3.7; Jude 1, 6 (*bis*), 13, 21.

8 But do not ignore this one fact, beloved, that with the Lord one day is as a thousand years, and a thousand years as one day. ⁹ The Lord is not slow about his promise as some count slowness, but is

---

8. The following verses show one way in which the early Church dealt with the delay in a literal End to the created order. Another was that of the Johannine school, that the 'hour' which is coming already 'is' (cf. Jn 4.23; 5.25). Eschatological fervour is a religious phenomenon, not primarily cosmological, and movements with particular hopes of this sort do not peter out with the disappointment of the original impetus. That the first Christians were aware that their faith was more than the expectation of an early end to history and a conviction of the instability of the creation is shown by 2 Peter's attitude here. The first Christians inherited such beliefs, as the pseudepigraphical literature and the DSS show. What made the difference was the coming of Christ, and the whole Judgment expectation was coloured by their experience of him. 'The end of all things is at hand' (1 Pet. 4.7) is a statement of the immediacy of God in Christ and of his action in the affairs of men.

beloved: the writer addresses the faithful who are puzzled about the delay of the End.

the Lord: God the Father; so in the Psalm and the Barnabas quotation below.

There is nothing unsophisticated about the notion that time has a different value to God from what it has to man. Whether it applies here or not is another matter, and the writer is vaguely aware of this. He suggests that God is not really slow, and then tacitly admits that he is by attempting to explain the delay in terms of his forbearance.

a thousand years as one day: cited from Ps. 90.4. In the *Epistle of Barnabas* 15.4f. the six days of creation are taken to mean 'that the Lord will make an end of everything in six thousand years, for a day with him means a thousand years'; and the rest on the seventh day means, 'When his Son comes he will destroy the time of the wicked one and judge the ungodly, and will change the sun and moon and stars'. The problem involved was felt by the Dead Sea Community: cf. 1QpHab on Hab. 2.3: *For still the vision is for an appointed time; it hastens to the period and does not lie'.* This means that the last period extends over and above all that the prophets said; for the mysteries of God are marvellous. *If it tarries, wait for it, for it will surely come: it will not delay:* This means the men of truth, the doers of the Law, whose hands do not grow slack from the service of the truth, when the last period is stretched out over them. For all the periods of God will come to their fixed term, as he decreed for them in the mysteries of his wisdom' (Millar Burrows' translation).

9. The delay of the End is a sign of God's clemency, to give men time to repent.

forbearing toward you, not wishing that any should perish, but
that all should reach repentance. ¹⁰ But the day of the Lord will come
like a thief, and then the heavens will pass away with a loud noise,
and the elements will be dissolved with fire, and the earth and the
works that are upon it will be burned up.

The Lord: once more God the Father: cf. verses 10 and 12 below, 'the day of the
Lord' is 'the day of God'. See on verse 15.
as some count slowness: the scoffers (verse 3) imply that God's delay is a sign
of impotence or carelessness.
toward you: some MSS read 'on your account'; others, 'toward us'.
not wishing that any should perish, but that all should reach repentance:
cf. Ezek. 33.11, 'Say to them, As I live, says the Lord God, I have no pleasure in
the death of the wicked, but that the wicked turn from his way and live'; and
1 Tim. 2.3f., 'God our Saviour, who desires all men to be saved'.
In Greek the notion of repentance is of a change of outlook, in Hebrew thought
a turning round and adopting a new way of life. The two are not incompatible.
The expression 'to reach repentance' is not used elsewhere in the New Testament.
10. the day of the Lord: see Am. 5.18ff, where the prophet reinterprets a
current concept (' Why would you have the day of the Lord? It is darkness, and
not light'); Jl 2.28ff. (note verse 31), quoted Ac. 2.17ff. See verse 12 below.
like a thief: the sentence 'the day of the Lord comes as a thief' appears in 1 Th. 5.2;
see also Mt. 24.43; Lk. 12.39; Rev. 3.3; 16.15. The notion of the sudden coming of
the Day does not well agree with its indefinite postponement in the previous
verse: cf. verse 15.
the heavens will pass away: see for the expression the isolated logion in Mk
13.31 (not directly connected with the *parousia*) and cf. Isa. 34.4; Rev. 20.11;
1 Enoch 91.16.
with a loud noise: that is, with a rushing sound, indicative of swiftness.
the elements: not the elemental spiritual powers of the universe (Gal. 4.3) closely
connected with the stars, but the stars themselves, or possibly the physical elements
of the universe: see the quotation from the *Sibylline Oracles* below.
will be dissolved with fire: 2 Peter returns to the doctrine unique to him in the
New Testament and the whole Bible: see above on verses 5–7.
the earth and the works that are upon it will be burned up: cf. 1 C. 3.13,
where the idea is different. 2 Peter envisages only destruction, not testing by fire.
See 1QH 3.29f.:
'When the rivers of Belial
burst their high banks
—rivers that are like fire . . .
a fire which consumes

11 Since all these things are thus to be dissolved, what sort of persons ought you to be in lives of holiness and godliness, 12 waiting for and hastening the coming of the day of God, because of which

---

all foundations of clay . . .
when the foundations of the mountains
become a raging blaze,
when granite roots are turned
to streams of pitch,
when the flame devours
down to the great abyss . . .' (cf. Mic. 1.3f.).
This is the translation of T. H. Gaster. Comparisons with the DSS are affected by the particular translation used. It is possible to make this passage more eschatological by casting it into the future and universalizing the terms; cf. Vermes:
'The torrents of Satan shall reach
to all sides of the world . . .
a consuming fire shall destroy . . .
and shall consume the foundations of the earth', etc.
A third translation, that of Millar Burrows, minimizes the eschatological tone by putting most of it into the past tense. (The Hymn, in any case, begins in the first person and so does not easily have a futuristic and universalizing interpretation.)
    Nearer to 2 Peter is the following from the *Sibylline Oracles* (a work influenced by the Babylonian conception of the Great Year):
'Then the elements of the world one and all shall be widowed, what time God whose dwelling is in the sky shall roll up the heaven as a book is rolled. And the whole firmament in its varied forms shall fall on the divine earth and on the sea: and then shall flow a ceaseless cataract of raging fire, and shall burn land and sea, and the firmament of heaven and the stars and creation itself it shall cast into one molten mass and clean dissolve' (III. 81–87 (Lanchester in Charles)).
will be burned up: Black points out that one sect of the Essenes (referred to in Hippolytus *Refut.* ix. 23 *sub. fine*) expects 'a judgment and conflagration' but believes that the souls of the righteous are imperishable. The text is corrupt. Variants include 'be not found' and 'disappear'. Conjectures include 'become fluid', 'be reduced to fire', 'be removed', 'be judged'.
    The whole picture of the 'day of the Lord' is cosmic, with none of the personal imagery of a man on the clouds.
    11. The writer uses the cosmic cataclysm not to inspire pity or fear but to underline the unimportance of everything except holy living.
lives of holiness and godliness: lit., holy ways of living and pieties.
    12. The author repeats the description of the End already given in verse 10.
hastening: or, 'earnestly desiring' (*RSV* margin). If the meaning is really 'hasten-

the heavens will be kindled and dissolved, and the elements will melt with fire! ¹³ But according to his promise we wait for new heavens and a new earth in which righteousness dwells.

14 Therefore, beloved, since you wait for these, be zealous to be found by him without spot or blemish, and at peace. ¹⁵And count

---

ing', the suggestion is that the holy lives will produce the End of this world in a manner reminiscent of the Jewish belief that absolutely faithful observance of the Torah for one day would bring the Messianic age. It is to be noticed that the End was an object of hope and not fear for the Christians, i.e., it was a religious matter and not purely catastrophic, as are modern visions of the End. In later years even Tertullian is found sometimes praying *pro mora finis*: *Apol.* 32, 39: *Ad. Scap.* 3.

coming: i.e., *parousia*, used here of 'the day of God' and not of a personal return of Christ. See on verse 10 (end).

the day of God: this is a variant of 'the day of the Lord' (verse 10). 'The great day of God the Almighty' occurs at Rev. 16.14, where it is followed by the words, 'I am coming like a thief': cf. verse 10 above. 2 Peter's language about the End is closer to that of certain Old Testament theophanies than to New Testament descriptions of the Second Coming of Christ. The coming of God in Mic. 1.3f., for example, is symbolized by the melting of mountains, and so on.

13. The Christians look for a new world in which righteousness will be the norm. This is the point of the destruction of the old, which must needs come to doom because it does not conform to the Christian way (cf. 2.2, 15, 21).

new heavens and a new earth: see Isa. 65.17; 66.22; Rev. 21.1, 27; also Rom. 8.21. The idea is commonplace in Jewish thought: cf. 1 Enoch 45.4f.; 72.1; 2 Baruch 32.6; 44.12; 57.2; Onkelos Targum on Dt. 32.12 ('in the world which God will renew'); Targum on Micah 7.14 ('in the world that will be renewed'); *Mekilta* on Exod. 16.25 ('the new world'), etc.

in which righteousness dwells: i.e., in which uprightness is at home.

THE LIFE WHICH LOOKS FORWARD TO A NEW WORLD 3.14–18

without spot or blemish: similar words are used of the blood of Christ in 1 Pet. 1.19, 'like that of a lamb without blemish or spot'; cf. 2 Pet. 2.13, where 'blots' (spots) and blemishes refers to the troublemakers, and Jude 24. The morality of 'blamelessness' is typical of the early Church (cf. Phil. 1.10; 1 Th. 3.13; 5.23; 1 Tim. 6.14; Jas 1.27).

and at peace: lit., 'in peace', with perhaps the suggestion that the blamelessness consists in peaceableness or produces the peace of God.

15. the forbearance of God. Paul expatiates on God's forbearance in the Epistle to the Romans 2.4; 3.25; 9.22; 11.22. In 3.25 he suggests that the Cross was

the forbearance of our Lord as salvation. So also our beloved brother Paul wrote to you according to the wisdom given him, ¹⁶ speaking of this as he does in all his letters. There are some things in them hard to understand, which the ignorant and unstable twist to their own destruction, as they do the other scriptures. ¹⁷ You therefore, beloved, knowing this beforehand, beware lest you be

---

the justification of this forbearance, which hitherto had looked like complacency: 'this was to show God's *righteousness*'. Rom. 2.4 asks, 'Do you presume upon the riches of his kindness and forbearance and patience? Do you not know that God's kindness is meant to lead you to repentance?' If 2 Peter means this here the word **salvation** bears the meaning 'the chance of salvation' or 'the means of salvation'. The word associated with Paul's doctrine of justification by faith and not works (which some perverted into a basis for antinomianism) is 'grace': cf. Jude 4 (=2 Pet. 2.1ff.).

our Lord: God the Father (cf. Rev. 11.15). The expression almost always refers to Jesus in the New Testament. From being the Aramaic address 'sir' (since *mar* always takes possessive suffixes) it became the name that is above every name— *kyrios*, Lord, being the Septuagint translation of YHWH, the ineffable divine name. But the title is used in the Apostolic Fathers for God the Father, and it is he who is in question in this chapter: 3.2, 5, 8, 9, 10, 12.

our beloved brother Paul: the writer rather ostentatiously stresses his assumed equality with the Apostle.

wrote to you: this does not mean that he wrote specifically to the addressees of this epistle. Paul's epistles were by now common property.

according to the wisdom given him: that is, 'in accordance with'; there is no depreciatory suggestion that Paul only wrote according to his lights.

16. speaking of this may refer to the dangers of falling away before the End (see verse 10 which is almost identical with 1 Th. 5.2). It may have to do with the disorderly conduct with which Paul had to deal at Corinth and the curious teaching at Colossae (Col. 2.16–19). Probably it recalls the Pauline teaching on grace (taken as the 'forebearance' of God: cf. the note on the previous verse) which was misunderstood by some as an invitation to licence: see Rom. 3.8; 6.1, 15 and the rest of this verse.

all his letters: the writer apparently knows of a corpus of Pauline epistles. Paul does, in fact, stress the ethical element in all his letters, which begin with doctrine and end with the ethical instruction which naturally proceeds from it.

there are some things in them . . . twist to their own destruction: see above on the first part of the verse.

the other scriptures: Paul's letters are by now 'scripture'.

17. The writer assumes once more the cloak of Peter as prophet.

carried away with the error of lawless men and lose your own
stability. ¹⁸ But grow in the grace and knowledge of our Lord and
Saviour Jesus Christ. To him be the glory both now and to the day
of eternity. Amen.

---

lose your own stability: cf. Jude 24. 2 Peter is also remembering 1 Pet. 5.10, 12.
18. Cf. 1.2b.

grow in . . . grace, etc.: the idea of growing into Christ occurs in Eph. 4.15, and
increasing in the knowledge of God in Col. 1.10 (cf. 1 Pet. 2.2). The meaning is
clear in the case of knowledge; growing in grace may mean increasing in favour
with God (cf. Lk. 2.52) or gaining more moral strength from him (cf. Jas 4.6).
The writer ends as he began on a note from 1 Pet. (5.12; cf. 2 Pet. 1.2 with 1 Pet.
1.1).

knowledge: the word is *gnōsis*, used at 1.5f. of a virtue, but here referring to that
acquaintance with Christ which is the Christian's privilege. 2 Peter usually uses
epignōsis: 1.2, 3, 8; 2.20.

our Lord and Saviour Jesus Christ: cf. 1.1 and the note there. But here
obviously only one person is referred to; the next sentence has 'To him', etc.

DOXOLOGY

This is conventional, except for the phrase 'the day of eternity' (cf. Rom. 16.27).
the day of eternity. Lit., a day of an age, i.e., an eternal day (cf. 1.20); see
Sir. 18.10, 'As a drop of water from the sea . . . so are a few years in the day of
eternity,' where 'the day of eternity' plainly means 'eternity'.

The doxology is addressed to Christ and not to God the Father (cf. 2 Tim. 4.18;
Rev. 1.6). It resembles that in Jude 25 in form, and, like it, recalls later examples.

INDEX

Abraham, 2, 9, 13, 16ff., 23, 41, 44, 45, 56, 77
Abraham, Testament of, see *Testament of Abraham*
Adam, 33, 72, 114, 119
Adam and Eve, Life of, 119
Andrews, 54
agapē (see also love feast), 68, 107, 115
Aḥiḳar, 101, 117
Aḳiba, 89
Albright, 18
Angels, 65, 66, 68, 70, 71, 72, 76, 83, 85–89, 91, 113, 115
Apocalypse of Moses, see Moses, Apocalypse of
Apocalypse of Peter, see Peter, Apocalypse of
Aristeas, 1, 4, 5, 54
Armenian version, 58
Assumption of Moses, see Moses, Assumption of
Athanasius, 98
Athenagoras, 76
Audet, 12

Balaam, 65, 66, 89
Bar Cochba, 77
Barnabas, Epistle of, 12, 14, 34, 36, 73, 76f., 93, 116, 121
Barr, 63
2 Baruch, 85, 124
bath ḳol, 110
Behm, 78
Belial, 122
Bengel, 38
Berosus, 120
Beyschlag, 39
Bigg, 78, 90
Billerbeck, see Strack and Billerbeck
Black, 123
Body, 47, 51, 108

Box, G. H., 30
Brownlee, 29
Buddhism, 48
Burrows, Millar, 121, 123

Cain, 66, 74, 86, 89
Carpocrates and Carpocratians, 71, 74, 87
Carrington, 3, 34, 54
Catechism, 2f., 12, 27, 33f., 107
chairein, 26
Charles, 6, 54, 68, 119, 123
Chenoboskion, see Nag Hammadi
Cicero, 1
Clement of Alexandria, 44, 60, 73, 75, 76, 88, 90, 93, 117
Clement of Rome (1 Clement), 11, 12, 13, 14, 18, 29, 44, 45, 51, 52, 53, 56, 58, 64, 73, 86, 107, 113, 114, 118
2 Clement, 12, 26, 29, 52, 58, 118
Coptic version, 93
Corpus Hermeticum, see Hermetic writings
Cynics, 1f.

Dalman, 41, 63
Dead Sea Scrolls, 4, 20, 22, 27, 29, 30, 32, 36, 39, 40, 41, 48, 52, 53, 74, 83, 87, 97, 112, 113, 116, 121, 122f.
'Deification', 95, 98, 106, 107
Democritus, 117
despotēs, 65, 84, 112
Diatribe, 1f., 2, 11, 18, 51
Dibelius, 2
Didache, 11, 13, 14, 29, 46, 62, 72, 73, 74, 75, 89, 92, 93, 112, 116
Didymus, 88
Diognetus, Epistle to, 1, 26
Dispersion, 1, 19, 26
Dodd, 3, 19, 32, 36, 37
Doresse, 74

Ebionites, 40
Egyptians, Gospel of the, 74, 93
Eldad and Modad, Book of, 12, 29, 52f., 54, 58, 118f.
Elliott-Binns, 60
End of the world, 96, 97, 118, 119, 120, 121ff., 125
1 Enoch, 5, 37, 41, 47, 55, 57, 68, 72, 75, 76f., 83, 85, 86, 87, 89, 90, 99, 113, 114, 120, 122, 124
2 Enoch, 60
Epictetus, 1
Epicurus, 1
Epiphanius, 71, 89
Erasmus, 51
Essenes, 74
Euripides, 72, 90
Eusebius, 19, 75, 99

Faith and works (see also Justification), 16f., 43, 95, 108, 117
Fire, destruction of the world by, 96, 97, 119, 120, 122, 123
Flood, 85, 113, 119, 120

Gamaliel, 119
Gaster, T. H., 53, 123
Gehenna, 14, 48, 87
Glasson, 67f.
gnōsis, 105, 107, 126
Gnosticism, 14, 49, 69, 71, 72, 74f., 75ff., 79, 83f., 85–89, 92, 93, 98, 105, 109, 117
Goodspeed, 27, 57
Great Year, 96, 119, 123
Grotius, 51

Ḥanina, Rabbi, 21, 31, 40
Hegesippus, 19f.
Hellenistic morality, 3, 46f.
Hermas, 11, 12, 13, 14, 26, 28, 29, 35, 36, 41, 52f., 53, 54, 55, 57, 60, 73, 107, 118

Hermetic writings, 32, 34, 37, 105, 107, 110
Hesiod, 67f., 72, 86, 113
Hippolytus, 71, 76, 87
Hippolytus, Canons of, 61
'Holiness Code' (Christian), 3, 33
Homer, 87
Hort, 33, 38, 82, 85

Ignatius, 14, 105, 112
Iranian doctrine, 30, 120
Irenaeus, 36, 51, 71, 74, 76, 77, 86, 87, 89, 92, 98, 99

James the Great, 14, 19f., 69, 74, 79
Jamnia, 15
Jeremias, J., 36, 78
Jerome, 75, 90, 93, 99
Joḥanan ben Zakkai, 15
Johannine writings, 6, 24, 37, 43, 45, 49, 73, 77, 82, 109, 121
Josephus, 19, 28, 85, 87, 113, 119, 120
Jubilees, 85
Jude Thomas, see Thomas
Justification, 16f., 39, 42, 43, 44f., 45, 125
Justin Martyr, 36, 44, 51, 58, 60, 76, 85, 109

Kabbalism, 74
Kilpatrick, 60
Kingdom, 40f., 59, 108
Kittel, G., 18, 63
Korah, 89
Koran, 56

Lanchester, 123
Law, 17, 19, 20, 23, 32, 33, 34f., 35, 36, 40, 41f., 46, 49, 55, 121, 124
logos, see Word
love feast, 68, 69, 115
Lucretius, 48
Luther, 21

Lyons and Vienne, Epistles to Churches of, 99, 107

Manson, T. W., 43
Marcosians, 87
Master, 65, 84, 112
Matthean tradition, 3, 6, 8, 14f., 18, 40, 42, 46, 49, 55, 58
Mayor, 38, 51
McNeile, 21, 22
Meir, Rabbi, 49
Metatron, 83
Michael, 86, 88, 115
Migne, 51
Moffatt, 27, 63
Moschus, 72, 90
Moses, 23, 29, 72, 88, 89, 100
Moses, Apocalypse of, 46
Moses, Assumption of, 68, 72, 84, 88, 91, 99, 115
Moule, C. F. D., 40
Muratorian Canon, 12, 73, 75
Mysteries, 109
Myths, 98, 99, 109

Nag Hammadi, 74, 100
Nairne, 35
Name of God, 35, 41, 125
Nicolaitans, 89
Noah, Book of, 68, 83

Odes of Solomon, 4, 28, 29, 35, 107
Ophites, 74, 86
Origen, 19, 73, 75, 85, 88, 99
Orphism, 44, 48
Oxyrhynchus Papyri, 93, 116

parousia (see also Second Coming), 10, 11, 14, 58, 59, 95, 96, 97, 109, 119, 122, 124
Perfect, 74, 86, 87
Persians, 30, 120
Peshitta version, 35, 47, 57, 101

Peter, Acts of, 100; Apocalypse of, 101, 113; Gospel of, 100; Preaching of, 100
Philo, 4, 5, 12, 16, 21, 31, 33, 34, 60, 85, 89, 119
Philoxenian Syriac, 93
Plato, 21, 26f., 30, 31, 32, 36, 42, 51, 52, 118
Plummer, 15
Poimandres, 32, 33, 107, 110
Polycarp, Martyrdom of, 73, 75, 83, 94
poor, 39f., 58
psychikos, 49, 71, 76, 82, 92

Rabbinic works, 4, 15, 21, 29, 30, 31, 36, 37, 40, 41, 42, 43, 45, 47, 48, 49, 50, 54, 55, 56, 57, 60, 63, 77, 83, 85, 89, 117, 119, 124
Righteous man, the, 23, 29, 40, 58
Ropes, 1, 2, 28, 34, 60, 63

Sahidic Coptic, 93
Second Coming, 10, 11, 14, 58, 59, 60, 90, 94, 95f., 97, 109, 110, 111, 119, 121, 122, 124
Selwyn, 3, 33, 54
Seneca, 4, 120
Servant, 26, 39
Seth, Sethites, 74, 86, 87, 89
Shekinah, 29, 38, 110
Sibylline Oracles, 96, 97, 122, 123
Sidebottom, 30, 35, 77
Simeon ben Johai, 30
Simon Magus, 71, 87
Simplicius, 48
Sodom and Gomorrah, 65, 66, 74, 86f., 89, 113, 114
Spirit, holy, 53, 71, 92, 106, 111f., 120
Spitta, 52
Stoics, 34, 120
Strack and Billerbeck, 29, 31, 39, 56
Streeter, 74
Syriac versions, 35, 47, 57, 93, 101, 110

Targums, 30, 41, 89, 124

Teaching of the Twelve Apostles, see
    Didache

Teles, 1f.

Temptation, 4, 22, 27

Tertullian, 62, 75, 76, 87, 90, 124

Testament of Abraham, 30, 32, 76, 89

Testaments of the Twelve Patriarchs, 5, 6,
    15, 28, 30, 31, 33, 37, 43, 48, 53, 54, 58,
    60, 85, 106

Thales, 120

Thomas, Gospel of, 93, 107

Thomas, Jude Didymus, 69, 79

Torah (see also Law), 17, 36, 49, 124

Transfiguration, 97, 99, 108, 109f., 110,
    111

Two ways, 12

Unnik, van, 20

Vermes, 123

Vulgate, 47, 110

Wells, 119

Westcott and Hort, 85

Weymouth, 27

Wheel of fate, 48

White, H. G. Evelyn, 68

Windisch, 63

Wisdom literature, 4, 23, 30, 33, 40, 49,
    50, 58

Word, 32f., 34, 35, 36, 110

World, the, 37, 40, 47, 52

Wrath, 33

Yeṣer hara', 30

Zoroastrianism, 31, 120

de Zwaan, 78